M000290376

Dolphins
in the Fire

A STORY OF YOUNG WOMEN AT SEA

From the Logbooks
of the Charter Fishing
Vessel, *Seawitch*

Captain Robert R. Singleton PhD

DOLPHINS IN THE FIRE: A STORY OF YOUNG WOMEN AT SEA

Copyright © 2018 Atlantic Publishing Group, Inc.

1405 SW 6th Avenue • Ocala, Florida 34471 • Phone 352-622-1825 • Fax 352-622-1875
Website: www.atlantic-pub.com • Email: sales@atlantic-pub.com
SAN Number: 268-1250

No part of this publication may be reproduced, stored in a retrieval system, or transmitted in any form or by any means, electronic, mechanical, photocopying, recording, scanning, or otherwise, except as permitted under Section 107 or 108 of the 1976 United States Copyright Act, without the prior written permission of the Publisher. Requests to the Publisher for permission should be sent to Atlantic Publishing Group, Inc., 1405 SW 6th Avenue, Ocala, Florida 34471.

Library of Congress Cataloging-in-Publication Data

Names: Singleton, Robert Randolph, 1937- author.
Title: Dolphins in the fire / by Captain Robert R. Singleton, PhD.
Description: Ocala, Florida : Atlantic Publishing Group, Inc, [2018] | Includes bibliographical references and index.
Identifiers: LCCN 2018010868 (print) | LCCN 2018017195 (ebook) | ISBN 9781620235935 (ebook) | ISBN 9781620235928 (paperback : alk. paper) | ISBN 1620235927 (alk. paper)
Subjects: LCSH: Fishing boats—Massachusetts—Cape Cod Bay—Anecdotes.
Classification: LCC SH452.9.B58 (ebook) | LCC SH452.9.B58 S56 2018 (print) | DDC 623.82/82—dc23
LC record available at https://lccn.loc.gov/2018010868

LIMIT OF LIABILITY/DISCLAIMER OF WARRANTY: The publisher and the author make no representations or warranties with respect to the accuracy or completeness of the contents of this work and specifically disclaim all warranties, including without limitation warranties of fitness for a particular purpose. No warranty may be created or extended by sales or promotional materials. The advice and strategies contained herein may not be suitable for every situation. This work is sold with the understanding that the publisher is not engaged in rendering legal, accounting, or other professional services. If professional assistance is required, the services of a competent professional should be sought. Neither the publisher nor the author shall be liable for damages arising herefrom. The fact that an organization or Web site is referred to in this work as a citation and/or a potential source of further information does not mean that the author or the publisher endorses the information the organization or Web site may provide or recommendations it may make. Further, readers should be aware that Internet Web sites listed in this work may have changed or disappeared between when this work was written and when it is read.

TRADEMARK DISCLAIMER: All trademarks, trade names, or logos mentioned or used are the property of their respective owners and are used only to directly describe the products being provided. Every effort has been made to properly capitalize, punctuate, identify, and attribute trademarks and trade names to their respective owners, including the use of ® and ™ wherever possible and practical. Atlantic Publishing Group, Inc. is not a partner, affiliate, or licensee with the holders of said trademarks.

Printed in the United States

PROJECT MANAGER: Danielle Lieneman
INTERIOR LAYOUT AND COVER DESIGN: Nicole Sturk

Dedication

This work is dedicated to Captain Luanne E. Paisley, and to all the wonderful young women who came and served.

They lent dignity to what sometimes would have been a Vulgar Brawl.

Table of Contents

To go fishing is the chance to wash one's soul with pure air, with the rush of the brook, or with the shimmer of sun on blue water. It brings meekness and inspiration form the decency of nature, charity toward tackle-makers, patience toward fish, a mockery of profits and egos, a quieting of hate, a rejoicing that you do not have to decide a darned thing until next week. And it is discipline in the equality of man — for all men are equal before fish.

Herbert Clark Hoover
(Hoover, 1946)

Foreword

At my home in Massachusetts, on my enclosed front porch, is a bookcase. It is rather unique in that it holds over 40 volumes of my captain logs. Each volume contains the year it was written on the binding. These are the logbooks from the fishing vessel, Seawitch, in which each day of her operation, details were recorded and documented. This bookcase is, in truth, a time machine; it opens its portals and lets us relive the past. These logs bring to life the days, the adventures, and the wonderful people (many of whom have now left us) of a time passed. The stories are about the amazing young women who were the first to work in the charter fishing boat industry. These are their stories and history, for they truly were the Dolphins in the Fire.

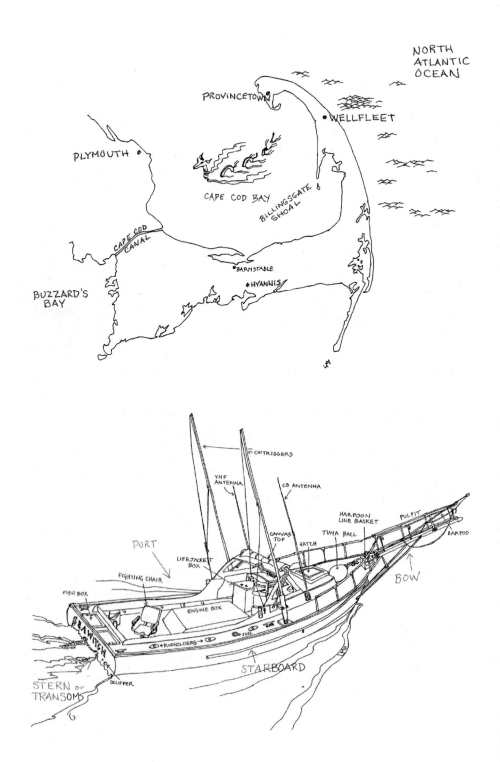

NORTH
ATLANTIC
OCEAN

PROVINCETOWN

•WELLFLEET

PLYMOUTH •

CAPE COD BAY

BILLINGSGATE
SHOAL

CAPE COD
CANAL

BUZZARD'S
BAY

•BARNSTABLE

•HYANNIS

OUTRIGGERS

VHF
ANTENNA

CB ANTENNA

HARPOON
LINE BASKET

PULPIT

PORT

CANVAS
TOP

HATCH

TUNA BALL

HARPOON

LIFEJACKET
BOX

FIGHTING CHAIR

BOW

FISH BOX

ENGINE BOX

RODHOLDERS

FUEL

STARBOARD

STERN or
TRANSOM

SCUPPER

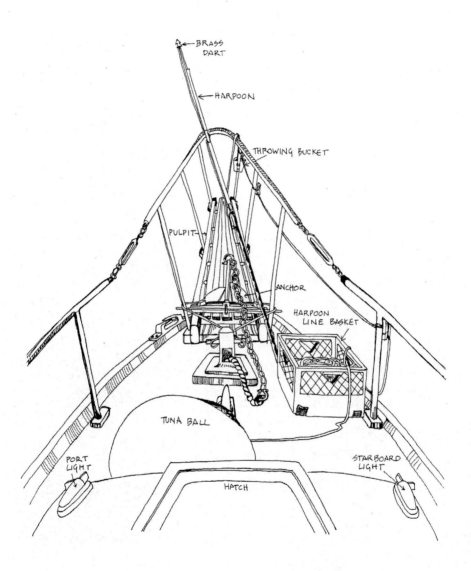

Introduction

〰〰〰〰〰〰

Many volumes have been written about the sea and the professionals who sail, search, and explore. There are tales of mystery, adventure, and battles with great fish. All of these things the reader will find in this work. These are the stories of people from every walk of life that one time or another came about on the charter boat, Seawitch for a day of fishing and adventure. This book is a salty hodge-podge of true stories taken from the log books and based on events covering a time span of 40 years. These stories are about the young women that were the first ever to work on a charter fishing vessel on Cape Cod Bay.

Captain Robert R. Singleton, PhD
Palmer, Massachusetts
2018

Chapter 1

A New Boat

The final decision to build a new Seawitch came suddenly during an afternoon charter in the late summer of 1973. The redhead from Cleveland looked up from the binnacle and gestured for me to come over. "We're heating up again," she said without expression.

"That's it," I grumbled. "Next spring we're gonna have a new boat." Earlier in the season I had replaced the old reliable, but worn out, gas engine with a new super-duper do-all gas engine that did nothing but lose us fishing time.

"If I ever see the inside of that damn piece of junk again, I'll quit," she said looking me in the eye and not smiling.

"OK," I said. "We're going to have a new fiberglass **hull** with a diesel and will put the best gear that we can find on her."

"You promise?" she asked.

I was about to answer, but she ran off and began explaining to the man in the fighting chair that he was not hooked to the bottom of the ocean, and if he didn't loosen the **drag** on the reel, that fish was going to pull him overboard and eat him. Besides that, if he lost the fish, she would **gaff** him instead. In a reasonable time, the fish was boated, and the smiling fisherman put his arms around her.

"Thanks," he said. "You're a good mate."

"Oh, it's true, it's true," she said rolling her green eyes heavenward and trying to hold back her laughter.

One of the younger members in the party reached into the bait tank and threw a mackerel at her, but she was too quick and ducked behind me for protection.

"You really mean it? A new boat!"

"Sure, I mean it."

"Can I come when you get it?"

"Yes," I told her, "and you can help choose some of the equipment."

Building a new Seawitch would mean a lot of planning, all my life savings, and a list of requirements for the builder, were as follows:

1. A sharp entry displacement hull constructed of reinforced fiberglass between 30 and 35 feet with a 10 to 12-foot beam; must be capable of carrying eight people through 3 to 5 feet seas at a cruising speed of 12 knots and a top speed of 15 knots, in case I had to make a run for it

2. A six-cylinder Marine diesel engine that had a long life expectancy and a fuel capacity of at least 100 gallons

3. Must be a total fishing machine; absolutely nothing ornamental or built for show

4. 18 feet of open cockpit space. The interior of the cabin would be designed as a tackle shop, with storage for 20 rods and reels, over a thousand **plugs**, **lures**, and **rigs**, and space for boxes of line, tools, and spare parts.

When I showed my requirements to Mr. Vanduser, a respected boat builder from across the Cape, he looked at me and handed back my list. "That's a real machine you want, and I'd love to build her for you, son, but I won't."

"Why?" I asked.

The old man stuffed his hands into his pockets and seemed to grow small inside his wind breaker.

"Why?" I asked again.

"'Cause," he replied flatly. "I don't want no son-of-a-bitch house carpenter working on a boat like that. All I got is one good man now and we're way behind on last year's orders."

I thanked him and asked if he knew of someone who could do the job.

"Not right off," he said. "But I may be able to find you someone. Let me get back to you in a day or so."

I felt a little let down that Mr. Vanduser's yard could not build my boat, but he was honest, and I would never doubt his judgment or question his reasons. He had been building boats for 60 years and his family had been in the business 100 years before him.

As it turned out, I didn't have too long to wait. Within a week I had chosen a hull design and settled on William Lauton, a builder from Portland, Connecticut. Our first meeting lasted only a short time. The builder, a huge man — almost 7 feet tall and weighed 300 pounds, all muscle — greeted me and my red-haired mate from Cleveland with a warm smile.

"I had a long talk with Mr. Vanduser from the Cape," he said. Hardly raising his voice above a whisper, "I want to build that boat."

I gave him my list of requirements and a pad of sketches, which he looked at thoughtfully for a few moments.

"I'll build her," Mr. Lauton said. "And if we need to make any changes, I'll call you."

We were given a tour of the yard and introduced to the master carpenter, his wife, and their three children, who had just immigrated from the Azures. The entire family had coal black hair, olive skin, and beautiful huge brown eyes. The contrast between them and my mate, with her combination of red hair, gold skin, and green eyes was astounding. The children could not keep from touching her. Cleveland loved the attention and good naturedly let the children play with her hair and gaze into her eyes. The smallest, about 5 years old, asked her mother in their native tongue if the nice lady was an angel. Everyone laughed, and Cleveland said no, that she was just a sophomore at Hampshire College, and that was one step in the other direction.

Mr. Lauton introduced us to his wife, who was 6 feet 2 inches tall, and their son, 6 feet 1 inch tall, and the family dog, which resembled a sort of stunted, fur-covered hippopotamus and bore the strange name of Mystone. I was inquiring of its origins when Junior blurted out that it eats cats. Dad came to Mystone's defense with, "Well, he's just the best damn watch dog we ever had."

And Mrs. Lauton backed him up with, "No one could be sure of that because no one has seen him do it."

Junior however, held his ground. "I saw him, two times!" he said. "Flea collars and all!"

Mrs. Lauton retreated a little, "Well, if he did, I'm sure they were just strays anyway."

And Mr. Lauton said he didn't give a damn what Mystone ate; his record as a watch dog was flawless, and, in reality, Mystone was just a friendly 135-pound puppy that was sometimes misunderstood.

Something in the back of my mind figured that the only way to stop that friendly puppy, once it made up its mind, was with a well-placed slug from a 308 Winchester.

As we were leaving, I told Cleveland that I never thought of my 6 foot, 220 pound stature as small, but somehow after meeting the boat builder and his family, I felt like a refugee from Tiny Town. I'm not sure she was paying attention as she was tossing her head side to side and singing, "We are the Munchkins of the lollipop guild, the lollipop guild."

As late fall drizzled into early winter, construction moved along with an occasional crisis and quite a few trips to the yard.

"Now Captain, what do we do about a **flying bridge?**"

"Nothing," I told Mr. Lauton. "I didn't want one."

"And just why the hell not?" he whispered down to me. "Cause I like to be with people. I don't want to isolate myself up on a bridge."

"You'll see better, and she'll look great with a bridge."

"That may be true," I explained, "but I like to be right down in the midst of the blood and the action. I enjoy teaching people how to fish, and a lot of my customers would feel let down if I didn't work with them. And as far as how she looks, well that isn't as important as how safe she is and how well she will fish."

"Don't worry about that," chimed in the master carpenter. "I'll build it to last a hundred years. And another thing, she will move through the water like El Gato, the cat. This boat is gonna catch more fish than any other boat you see, you just wait."

At the time, I knew that his new boat would be good, but it wasn't until the following spring that the carpenter's words struck home. She wasn't just good, she was fantastic! In almost 20 years of working sports fishing boats of every description, I never had one that could catch fish like this one. Her knifed edged passage through the water was silent and left very little turbulence and hardly any **wake** when **trolling**. She could cat foot into a school of feeding stripers or bluefish without spooking them or breaking up their feeding. Her ability to turn and work big game fish was simply amazing. It didn't take me long to get the feel of this boat, for she has her own personality of a sweetheart. She wasn't just a nice handling boat on the sea; she behaved and worked like she was part of the sea.

However, early in her construction someone made a mistake; thankfully it was one that I would never regret. There was absolute astonishment on everyone's face when the cardboard was torn from the side of this huge wooden packing crate. All of us had expected to see a conservative six-cylinder motor. What stood menacing before use was the biggest, most powerful looking eight-cylinder diesel I had ever seen.

The carpenter said something in his native tongue that loosely translated to, "What the hell is that?"

My own words were unprintable. The builder and the rest of the yard crew chimed, "Oh shit!" in unison.

Everyone's first thought was that this monster was too big and too powerful for this boat, and I was about to agree when the strongest smile came across the face of the builder.

"You're not thinking what I think you're thinking?" I asked Mr. Lauton.

Suddenly everyone except me had the same smile. Only now people were running in search of slide rules and tape measures.

"You guys have got to be kidding me!" I said. "We can't put that — " I cut my sentence short, as no one was listening. They had gone into a huddle that broke every few seconds when someone scurried away to the monster with a ruler or something and returning with the same possessed smile.

Since I wasn't needed, I took a walk and visited Mystone, who was in jail for a few days. He had been muzzled and cabled to a fork lift inside a storage shed. It seems that several small animals and house pets in the area were missing, including two Doberman puppies over in the next boat yard. I believe all that was left was a few paws and part of one hide, but I hadn't viewed the remains. And as to what had gotten at them, no one could be sure, but it was agreed that Mystone should be locked up for his own safety. Mr. Lauton didn't want whatever had gotten the Dobermans to get Mystone.

"You're just a poor misunderstood old puppy," I said as he sprawled beside the fork lift.

He lifted his head as if in recognition, and I caught sight of a dull yellow eye following me from behind a mop of matted hair. There was something familiar yet almost prehistoric about that eye. However, it took a while before I remembered that I had seen one like it somewhere in a painting of a Tyrannosaurus Rex.

When I returned, the crew had the engine unpacked and buckled to a **chain fall**.

"Well Captain, she's going to be just fine," said Mr. Lauton.

"OK, so it fits — but what about weight and fuel consumption?"

"Don't worry about the weight. That hull can handle it." He assured. "And as far as what she burns, you'll use less fuel because you'll never need to open her up and you'll never use all she can give."

I wasn't sure what the hell he was saying, but in time, I was happy. I abided by his decision. That big wonderful engine has never given us a moments trouble in over 10 summers of continuous operation. Almost 11,000 hours of working sea time without an overhaul or a major repair. And she still doesn't use oil.

It was a warm, bleached out April morning in 1974 when we rolled the new Seawitch out of the shed. Friends and customers of mine came from all over the eastern United States to see their new fishing platform and toast her with champagne.

The sign painter said something that morning as he finished the **transom** that I'll never forget. "How many boats have you had with this name?" he asked.

"Three," I told him. "This is the fourth."

"Well, I'm glad you didn't want any numbers after the name. I think it would spoil it."

I nodded in agreement.

"You know son," he added, "I've seen a lot of boats, but I've never seen one as simply beautiful as this one. She looks like a Seawitch. The name really fits."

Chapter 2

Dolphins in the Fire

Sometimes we are too busy with our lives to pause along the way and enjoy the things God has created. However, seeing the world through the eyes of my grandchildren and the young people around me is always a delight. It's like I have been given a second chance to be part of their wonder of discovery.

This story has a timeless quality about it. Yet, it is the story of God's creation, and the joy of discovering and being part of it.

As Eugene Field wrote:

> *Wynken, Blynken, and Nod one night*
> *Sailed off in a wooden shoe, -*
> *Sailed on a river of crystal light,*
> *Into a sea of dew.**

I have always found it difficult to say goodbye to old friends and customers, but a three-day charter of tuna and blue fishing out of Provincetown left my mate, Annabelle, and I with no clean clothes, a depleted tackle inventory, and the Seawitch overdue for an oil change. It was time to go home. The sun was well below the horizon as we rounded Long Point, and

---

*Field, Eugene, and Ron Berg. *Eugene Field's Wynken, Blynken and Nod*. New York: Scholastic, 1985. Print.

twilight was falling as I thought about our labors of the past bright and busy three days.

"Provincetown," said Annabelle, looking back at the lights that were beginning to wink along the shoreline. "I never come away from that place feeling the same."

"Why's that?" I asked.

"I don't know. It's always different, I guess."

"Well, I suppose it's different things to different people," I said. "What do you feel about it now?"

Annabelle took off her Miller Beer baseball hat and threw it in the cabin.

"It was like being at a carnival today. Like a circus," she said. "What do you think about it?"

"I think what I always think. I put it into a category years ago, and I haven't had a reason to change my opinion since."

"And what's that?"

"Baghdad," I said.

Annabelle bit her lower lip, then broke into a smile. "Like a Persian market. Like Sinbad the Sailor, right?"

I nodded in agreement.

"Like camels in the sand dunes. Like ..."

"That's enough," I said. "You got it."

Annabelle stepped up on the life jacket box and leaned over the windshield. "You know," she said, "After a while, sometimes it's nice not having people aboard. I'm glad they stayed behind."

I didn't reply but gave her a knowing glance. I switched on our running lights and watched the sea turn from burned copper into deep purple as Provincetown disappeared into our wake and the events of the past three days entered our memories. Light was going now except for a thin shot of orange that hung in the southwest like a beacon left behind to point our way home, but it too, would soon fade and leave us alone with only the deep reassuring sound of the engine and the soft, red glow of our own deck lights, and of course, our thoughts.

I have spent thousands of nights at sea, all somehow the same and yet, strangely, all different. Staring into the darkness beyond the bow, the ghosts of other days and the memories of the years step swiftly and quietly into view. Visons, dreams, laughter, and tears, and the faded faces of those I loved and left behind somehow come to me in this loneliness. They are with me on the deck, kissing me as soft spray, then fade, passing into the wake. Stepping back with the darkness into their place and time, while the future, my future, is out there just beyond the bow, sailing ahead, yet always within the slam of a piston, the turn of a prop, or the beat of a heart away.

"Look at the stars," Annabelle said, pointing overhead, bringing me back to reality and the present.

I look up to see Altair, Deneb, and Vega twinkling down and the faint outline of their constellations beginning to take shape for their night ride across the summer sky.

"Do you know the names of the stars?" she asked, not turning from her gaze.

"Sure. Would you like me to show you?" I offered.

"Yeah, but I got to do a few things first," she said, hopping off the life jacket box and disappearing below.

I looked ahead as the small, sentinel stars began to post themselves along the rim of the horizon. The water bearer poured his water, the goat ate, and the archer drew his bow at the scorpion, who was reaching out for the scales. The eagle and the goose were now full and in flight midway along the star stream of the Milky Way, and we pushed along beneath it all at 8 knots, seemingly motionless in a raven-black sea.

When she came back on deck, Annabelle was lost in my oversize turtleneck sweater that Cleveland had knitted for me. It covered her from her nose to well below her knees.

"You look like a shmoo," I said.

"What's a shmoo?" she questioned, taking her seat on the life jacket box.

"A comic book character created by Al Capp. You know, in Li'l Abner."

"No, don't know. Maybe it was before my time. Was it like Peanuts or Doonesbury?"

"No," I said, feeling just a bit older. "Dog Patch was nothing like that."

"What?"

"Never mind," I said

"What's that one?" she asked, pointing in the direction of the Scorpion.

"Antares."

"And that one over there?"

"That's Arcturus," I answered. "And the big bright one over our heads is Vega."

"How come that one over there doesn't twinkle?"

"Because it's Jupiter, and planets don't twinkle." I explained.

"I love Star Trek. I had a crush on Mr. Spock when I was a kid," she admitted.

I laughed at her and told her that being on the uphill side of 18 years didn't exactly qualify her for Medicare, but she countered, "Oh well, you know what I mean."

I did and smiled back at her.

"Let's pretend this is a starship and we're going through the galaxy," she said after a time. "I could be Uhura or somebody and you're Kirk."

"All right," I agreed. "I'll give you a 10-minute tour of the summer sky and its constellations."

"How fast are we going to go?"

"How about 200 times the speed of light?" I said, turning the bow towards Hercules, the Dragon, and the Great Bear.

"I see the Dipper," she said. "Now find the North Start for me. It's the bright one with the two small ones on each side, right?"

"Wrong. That's Kochab and the Guardians," I said, taking her hand, and pointing it at Polaris, "But you were close. Just use the two big stars that make the lip of the Dipper as pointers and you'll find it every time."

"I read your navigation book, but I didn't pay much attention to the star part," she admitted with a giggle.

"Well, that's it for you," I said. "I'm going to give you to Orion slave traders, and they'll sell you to some fish cleaners in Pisces."

"I'm a Pisces. Show me where Pisces is," she asked, still giggling.

"Warp 200, Mr. Sulu," I said, swinging the bow through Cassiopeia, Andromeda, and straightening the course for the center of the Great Square.

"That small circle of stars on the horizon is one of the fish and that little delta is another," I said, pointing.

Annabelle remained silent and watched the small stars that were her constellation slide up on our starboard as I corrected our course for home.

"You know, Capt., we really are a starship, aren't we?" I mean, we really are going through space and the stars, aren't we?"

"Yes, ma'am. We sure are," I said, thinking about a conversation I once had with my 15-year-old son, Arthur.

"Look Dad," he said, "even if we do reach light speed, it will still take us generations to reach the stars. I believe we can find a better way."

"And just how do you suppose we do that?" I asked. "I mean, there are laws of physics that can't be broken."

Arthur put his arm around my shoulder and looked at me with a benevolent and somewhat forgiving smile. "I don't want to complicate that conversation, Father, but I will state that there are theories and I personally think that it can be done by trans-dimensional crossovers. The problem with most people is that they keep thinking in terms of speed and time when what they should be thinking about is cutting under the time-space curve and traveling through space, but not time. It's sort of like cutting through the backyard to get home instead of going around the long way and coming in the front door."

"A back-door theory," I said.

"Yes, Dad, if that will help you understand it. As a matter of fact, I got this idea for a light powered transfer engine that just may do the job once we can find a way to slip under the curve and navigate safely. I call it a Wasparian Star Transfer engine. I came up with the name from some of the factors I'm working with, like wave space, etc."

Arthur had once again left me with my mouth open and feeling, I believe, somewhat the same way as **Mr. Wright** *felt about his two sons, Orville and Wilbur, tinkering away in his bicycle shop.*

Annabelle left her seat and went and knelt in the fighting chair while I stared out at the stars that were mirrored ahead in the black sea. They appeared to tumble in our **bow** wake, then race along the **gunnels**, rolling and falling into the **prop wash**, which tore them apart into a million tiny sparks of light that fell together again in the fading distance as if they had never been disturbed.

While watching this, it wasn't hard to imagine that the sound of the diesel was the sound of the huge Wasparian Star drives hurtling us through the cosmos, through the very fabric of space, beyond the realm of time as we knew it. I mean, after all, hadn't Annabelle and I just completed a 10-minute tour that had taken us through half the galaxy? God only knows what Arthur and kids like him would come up with given the time, the tools, and the freedom from war, want, and hunger. Who knows, perhaps he and other little nerdy **eggheads** like him would soon strap themselves into ships and split the clouds of Magellan.

Annabelle returned after a while and curled up on the life jacket box, almost hidden in my sweater.

"Did you take a nap?" I asked. "You were back there a long time."

"No, I had some thinking and catching up to do."

"Catching up?"

"Yup, Capt., catching up. I haven't said my prayers for days. We've been so busy, and I just forget sometimes. You know how it is."

"Sure," I said. "I hope you put in a good word for me?"

"I do all the time, even for the other boats, too."

"We all need it. Thank you," I said.

"My mom worries a lot. She said I'd be better off working in a summer camp for the summer."

"What do you feel?"

"Heck! I wouldn't give this job up. I never loved anything so much in my life. I wish I could do it forever."

"You would get tired of it after a time." I explained, "And want to do something else."

Annabelle slid off the life jacket box and joined me at the wheel. "I would not," she said, staring up at me.

I put my arm around her shoulder. "You'll be doing lots of wonderful things in your life," I explained. "You've got school to finish, and I'm sure you'll want a family someday."

"You're wrong, Captain," she said pushing my arm away. "How long have you been doing this?"

"Almost 30 years," I answered.

"And you have a family, don't you?"

"Yes, ma'am."

"Now tell me honestly, would you really want to do anything else? I mean, you can have a family and everything like that and do this too, can't you?"

"I'm wrong," I said, backing down. "You got me."

"Permission to gloat?"

I nodded at the laughing face. "Go ahead," I said. "You deserve it."

"Can I have the rest of that hug now?" she asked still beaming.

"Why not?" I answered, reaching around my blue sweater and squeezing.

A small white light several miles to the southeast of us flashed at three second intervals, marking the beginning of Billingsgate Shoals. To the left of it, I could see the slow-turning red, green, and white lights of six or seven bass boats working its northern edge.

"We're half-way home," I said to Annabelle, who was again on her seat, star gazing.

She turned to speak to me, but something aft caught her attention. "Oh! Oh my God! Look!" she squealed.

I spun around to see that our pro and wake had turned into brilliant blue and white fire.

"What is it?" she demanded. "What is it?"

I had neglected to tell Annabelle about this phenomenon, and it was a few seconds before I recovered from laughter and my own surprise.

"Fire in the water," I managed, as she raced to the transom, I'm sure, not believing her eyes.

"What makes it?" she shouted.

I looked ahead to see that not only our stern was lit up, but twin ribbons of white and blue sparks were streaming away from the bow, and that both funnels were trailing deep purple and blue fire.

"Have a good look first, then I'll tell you all about it," I yelled as she bent over the bait tank and stared into the prop wash.

Within a few seconds, she was back on her feet and touring the deck. "It's everywhere!" she cried, obviously delighted and swinging her arms about. "It's like Winslow Homer."

"That's right," I said after a moment, remembering his famous painting of the herring fisherman. "You got it."

"Well, what makes it?"

"Small organisms, mostly plankton, in the sea," I said. "When they get churned up, they light up because of a chemical reaction. The waters of the Bay are warmer than the waters off Provincetown, and these organisms are found mostly in warm waters. That's why we didn't see them until we go well down into the Bay."

"Is it always this bright?"

"No, not all the time like this," I answered. "Some nights all you see is a few sparks, and once in a while you get a night like this."

A school of sand eels rose up in front of us in a blue cloud, then showered sparks in a domino effect that spread out for 50 yards in front of us. Annabelle was speechless at the sight of this, as suddenly it appeared as if someone beneath the sea had turned a flood light on.

"Any motion in the water at all will produce light," I explained as the school parted and passed under us.

"Were those sand eels?"

"Sure."

"Gosh! All you see in the daytime are the ones on top. I didn't know the schools were so big."

"Tip of the iceberg. Remember?"

"Gosh! What was that?"

"Probably bass," I said, as several pale blue contrails materialized in the blackness to the starboard.

"It's better than day time. You can see everything! Everything that moves!"

"Sure," I said, "but a lot of times it works to our disadvantage."

"Why?"

"Well, for obvious reasons. Bait fish won't move as much, and this slows down the whole feeding chain."

"Just not all the time, right?"

"No, not all the time. I've seen blue fish feed all night long on a night like this. It all depends if the fish can find the bait and stay with it. The kind of bait it is also matters."

As I was speaking, a flock of rafting gulls, which were lying along our course line, flopped into the air with dazzling effect. Feet, tail feathers, and some wing tips dripped sparks as the immediate horizon puddled blueish-green fire.

"Their bellies are glowing! Their bellies are glowing!" said Annabelle, pointing in the air.

"That stuff sticks," I said. "Remember Homer's picture?"

I slowed down the throttle to trolling speed. "Go drag the mop in the wash for a second," I ordered.

Within a minute Annabelle was playing Tinker Bell, using the mop to make streaks of light all her own.

"You're right. It sticks, but not like on the gulls," she said, displaying the spark-dripping mop.

"If you left it in for a while it would." I said, pushing the throttle, and checking the compass.

"Do you think there's life out in the stars like us, Capt.?"

I thought for a moment. "Sure," I said. "If there isn't, God sure made a lot of empty ground."

Annabelle hopped up on the life jacket box and leaned over the windshield. "I wonder what it will be like when we meet them for the first time."

I was about to say I didn't know when a huge **phalanx** of bluish-white fire crossed our bow with incredible speed, made a wide sweep around our starboard horizon, and eventually turned into our wake.

"Like right now!" I shouted above the sound of the diesel. "Like right now!"

"What is it?" Annabelle shouted back.

"Life," I said. "Warm, intelligent life, and it's coming to meet us."

The phalanx divided in the wake, sending sparks showering back on the blue funnels of iridescence, and in seconds, they were with us.

"They're dolphins!"

Around us, beneath us, and crisscrossing the bow ahead of us, they played with us. Diving, breathing, and spiraling through the fire. They took away our loneliness and filled our hearts with joy as they escorted us along the silent mirrored star stream, along the Milky Way, and all the long way home.

Chapter 3

The Beer Bust, or The Trip That Never Was

The following sad short story is dedicated to the officers and men of a certain Western Massachusetts fire department and to their loving wives and girlfriends that made it possible. It is without question that these dear ladies have added a new dimension to the time-honored cliché: "Hell has no fury like a woman's scorn and vengeance is a dish best served cold and again. Just you wait **Henry Higgins**. Just you wait."

This drama began on a sweltering Sunday morning in late July of 1980. What was supposed to be a two-boat trip, myself and the 'Tramp,' had changed a few days prior. I was informed that one boat was all that was needed, and the Seawitch was it. When I arrived at the harbor a half an hour early, I wasn't surprised to find everything aboard, set, and ready. As Annabelle, my mate for the season, was one of those super-efficient people who made any work seem effortless. She was one of the most fastidious clean freaks I have ever known. All one had to do was point out once what had to be done and Anabelle had it covered. Annabelle was always cheerful, helpful, and tolerant to all people. She always tried to make the best out of any situation, regardless of how unusual it was. And this day would put that to the test.

The high morning tide had filled the basin with clean, clear water. She, along with several mates from other boats, glided and splashed together like a group of playful otters out for their morning swim.

"Is it time yet?" she shouted as I made my way down the ramp.

"No, you can swim a few more minutes." I said as the troop slid gracefully underneath the **pulpits** and around the **finger peers**.

"I think I'll get out. Will you hose me down Captain?"

"Sure." I said as the whole troop splashed up to my dock.

"You better turn your head, Captain," one of the boys said laughing. "We're going to get out too and some of us are skinny dipping."

"You're supposed to do that at night. Not in broad daylight!" I said, turning the hose toward the laughing faces.

"Aw Capt., there ain't nobody up this early, and if someone came and said something we can put our suits on in the water."

I wasn't about to give this group of young men and women an argument as there was some logic in what they were saying. It was also easy to remember that I too was young once. I held the spray toward the rear of the dock and turned my head away from the sounds of the squeals, giggles, and laughter as the mates tumbled onto the platform into the spray of cold fresh water.

"Who's coming today, Captain?" Annabelle shouted from inside the cabin.

I waited until she was back on deck before answering her. "Firemen," I said, "And you'll find them a pretty interesting group."

"Oh, I bet they love to fish. I'm sure we'll have lots of fun."

"Well I've had them a couple of times before and they sure enjoy themselves, no matter what. They don't care if they fish or not."

"I can understand that," she said, brushing her hair. "It's just nice being on the sea in hot weather."

"Well Lady Godiva, that's not the point I was trying to make, "I said, "But that's part of it."

Annabelle shriveled up her nose and looked up into my face. "Well don't be a tease Capt. Are they going to fish or are we going for a boat ride?"

"We're pretending to go fishing so we can go for a boat ride, so they can do what they want to do. Get it?"

"OK, but what is it they want to do?"

"Eat, play cards, and drink beer. Mostly drink beer."

Annabelle started to laugh but caught herself. "We don't allow drunks on board. I don't understand. Are you changing the rules?" She said, shriveling up her nose again.

"No young lady, I'm not. They don't get drunk. At least I've never seen one of them drunk."

"Well, I guess if they don't drink that much," she said reasoning.

"Wrong again, sweetheart," I said. "They guzzle it."

"And they don't get bombed?"

"No, they don't get bombed. They just get feeling sort of pleasant and happy. You'll find them very polite."

Annabelle's face brightened. "Gosh, they sure sound unique," she said.

Unique just wasn't the word to describe this crew, I thought. It would be like calling the South Pacific a lake. Words like unique, unusual, and different would have to step aside in place of stronger stuff, like leviathan, behemoth, and majestic to explain the likes and carryings-on this crew of firemen. These men were the stuff that legends are made of and their names and deeds were heralded in every Berkshire village and town.

First of the crew was Six-Pack Parker, a red-eyed little man of 235 pounds who had hands like a rock crusher. Six-Pack had once saved the lives of two people by driving through the cracked ice of a small pond and ripping the back door off a Buick.

Six Pack's partner was Hops Henniger, a quiet, introspective man, who collected rare beer bottles and wrote fan letters to his favorite brew masters.

The others in this party, which I came to call the Fire House Five, were Barrels Barrette, Funnels Flanagan, and last but not least, the most colorful character of them all: the awesome Suds Sadolski. Suds was a massive figure who weighed over 325 pounds, stood 6 feet 5 inches and quoted Shakespeare. He had the appetite of Henry the VIII, the disposition of **Falstaff,** and the protective qualities of a female grizzly. Suds hated violence of any kind and was always quick to stop any bar room fight or brawl. This and their Herculean thirst for beer made him and his friends the darlings of the tavern set.

The Fire House Five planned their outing with military precision and spent plenty of time paying careful attention to the details. Travel arrangements and boat bookings were always made well in advance. And about as much work went into the choice and preparation of the menu as to the final choice of beverages. As far as the menu was concerned, dear reader, let's forget the word calorie, as it had an alien sound with no meaning to these men. It was something that foolish people like myself had to worry about, not these Titans.

They always brought hampers full of delights like smoked turkey, home-grown sugar cured ham, canisters full of tangy potato salad, rings of wonderfully pungent kielbasa, and fragrant stuffed sausages. There were jars of pickled eggs, pickled pig's feet, olives, peppers, and loaves of fresh home-made bread. And of course, one or two boxes of large black cigars that gave off a blue-yellow smoke that reminded one of being stalled behind a city bus in the **Callahan Tunnel**. All of these were mere appetizers and only led to the gate of their garden of joy, for it was the contents of four huge ice packed coolers that held their pièce de résistance: the beer. These were filled with bright shiny cans from Holland, Denmark, Canada, and Milwaukee, and several old-fashioned brown quart bottles that came from a supposedly respectable lady bootlegger from the Berkshires. She was affectionately referred to by them as 'our dear Mrs. Willard.'

Annabelle's only mistake of the day came shortly after the fire house five stepped from their van.

"Hi, I'm Annabelle," she said cheerfully. "Can I carry your gear to the boat?"

There was about two seconds of stone silence followed by a full minute of roaring laughter as poor bewildered Annabelle looked on.

"No, thank you child," said Hops wiping the tears from his eyes.

"Our gear's a bit heavy, but there is one thing you can do for us today, isn't there boys?"

"Sure thing. You bet," they all said looking down at the smiling Annabelle.

"You can be Keeper of the Key. Right boys?"

"Yeah, that's right," they all repeated.

"Begin the ceremony," said Funnels.

"Ta da ta da. The ceremony," they all repeated in a Three Stooge-like fashion.

Annabelle was lifted off her feet by Suds with about as much effort as it would take to lift a tea cup and deposited her on the hood of my pickup. Hops reached into the van and retrieved a lovely hand carved box and marched briskly up to the rank that had formed in front of Annabelle.

Suds and Barrels stepped to the opposite sides of Hops who held the chest at arm's length.

"Ta da ta da," they all sang.

"We hereby appoint thee — aw, what's your name, honey?" said Hops.

Annabelle giggled out of control.

"Calm yourself child," said Suds, reaching out and squeezing Annabelle's toe.

"I'm Annabelle," she managed to blurt out between sobs of laughter.

"Ta da ta da. We hereby appoint Annabelle, Keeper of the Key."

Barrels snapped open the box which was lined with green velvet and Suds lifted out a beautiful sterling chain necklace from which a solid gold can opener dangled.

Annabelle's eyes filled with wonder. "Oh my! It's beautiful!" she exclaimed breathlessly. "It's a can opener?"

"A church key," corrected Six Pack. "And your job is to see that all the bottles and cans are opened correctly."

"But you don't need an opener for that. They're all pop tops and spin offs."

"Not all child," said Suds as he dropped the necklace around Annabelle's neck. "There are a few hold outs and we're always prepared, right boys?"

"Right," they all repeated. "We're always prepared."

The Keeper of the Key was brought aboard, sitting cross-legged atop a cooler carried by Suds and Funnels.

"Well I see you have found a new position in life," I said, bowing as Anna-belle held out the gold key for my inspection.

"Yes, you may call me Lady Annabelle, Keeper of the Key," she said, sliding off her throne.

"I'll call you Shark Bait if you drop that thing overboard," I said, winking at Suds who was lifting another cooler aboard.

"No, we won't do that unless she spills a beer," he said laughing.

"I thought you fellows had two boats booked for today?"

Suds took the third cooler from Six Pack and pushed it under the starboard gunnel. "We did, but we decided not the bring them after all," he said straightening up. "I guess we had a moment of weakness or something."

"Weakness?" I said. "I don't understand."

"Well Capt., I don't know how it got started, but when we were talking about coming down one of the girls said how nice it would be if we brought our wives, friends, and some of the kids along. And before you know it, ev-eryone is making arrangements. Some people were looking for babysitters and we were finding it more complicated trying to get everything set, so we said the hell with it. We told them we'd bring them down another time. They didn't like it, but we'll make it up to them later."

I nodded my head as there wasn't too much I could say, but Annabelle managed to express her view as well as mine by announcing to the Fire House Five that they should have brought the girls along because she knew that they would have a good time. And ladies like to fish just as much as men.

"I'm sure you're right," said Hops diplomatically. "But we kind of like to relax when we get a little time off. And with the kids and women, it some-times proves to be a grind."

"Fiddlesticks!" Annabelle said holding her ground. "You would still have a good time and it's worth the trouble."

Barrels ended the confrontation by grabbing Annabelle by the waist and lifting her up to Sud's height.

Suds reached out and gently rubbed his thumb on Annabelle's turned up nose. "Your tip today will be reduced by 10 percent if I hear anymore," he said.

Annabelle squealed out an apology between sobs of laughter, along with a promise to keep her mouth shut.

"My! What a bright intelligent child you are," said Suds. "We shall increase your tip by 20 percent. Right men?"

"30 percent it shall be."

"Don't forget that 5 percent bonus if she is a good Keeper of the Key," added Hops.

"That's right," they all agreed. "But only if she does a good job."

"I'll do a good job," Annabelle said as Barrels lowered her gently to the deck, "But I don't know what to do other than open cans."

"Fear not, my child," said Suds. "I shall endeavor to instruct you in your task so that you may perform your duties with cheerfulness and dispatch, and since you have proven to us that you are indeed intelligent, we feel that you will surely overcome any intricacies of the aforementioned burden."

Annabelle's jaw went slack as she stared up at the fireman. "Gosh," was all she could manage.

A benevolent smile spread across Sud's face. "It is with this knowledge in mind," he continued, "That I fell it appropriate that we not break tradition and continue our practice of advance gratuitous remuneration. Agreed men?"

"Agreed," they all said nodding at the keeper of the key.

"Goodness!" Annabelle whispered looking at Barrels. "What did he say?'

"He said we'll give you your tip in advance because we may forget to later."

"Oh, I think I understand," she said grinning anew.

Suds took out his billfold and removed an envelope which was marked trip money and took out a new $100 bill from it. He presented it to Annabelle. The envelope was then passed to me. "We always like to pay in advance."

Annabelle was mesmerized by the new $100 bill. "I can't take this," she said offering the bill back to Suds. "It's just too much."

Suds waved the bill off with a doff of his hand. "Thinking nothing of it. You'll earn it in good time."

"But I still don't know what to do?"

"Now child. Worry not, for I now will impress upon you your duties as Keeper of the Key."

Annabelle squished up her nose and gave Suds an 'I'm listening as hard as I can' look as Suds pointed to two large hampers that sat on the engine box. "These," he said, "contain the quintessence of epicurean delights."

"What's that?" questioned Annabelle.

"Food," answered Hops. "Anytime anybody wants something, dig it out."

"OK," she said breaking into a grin. "Something in there smells wonderful."

"Kielbasa," said Hops.

"Ka–, ka–, what?"

"A big Polish hot dog," said Six-Pack.

"Gosh. Can I try some?"

"Certainly," said Suds, "But first let me bring your attentions to these four large coolers that line the inside perimeters of the vessel."

Annabelle was giving Suds her look again.

"The coolers contain many bottles and cans of certain golden elixir which is nectar to the Gods."

"Beer," said Annabelle.

"You got it," said Funnels.

"And I open beer."

"Right, sweetheart. Every time someone sits down an empty, you make sure that when his hand goes up again he has a full one in it. Got it?"

Annabelle stared at the four coolers. "Boy!" she said. "That's a lot of beer. Which one do I start with?"

Suds pointed to a baby blue cooler under the port gunnel. "This one. We always start with the pilsner. Right, gentlemen?"

"Right," they agreed.

"Yes, a pilsner is a fine way to greet the morning," added Hops.

Suds looked at his watch thoughtfully, "Time, gentlemen?"

"Time," they agreed.

"Keeper of the Key, you may serve the pilsner," ordered Suds.

At this time in my narrative, dear reader, I must inform you that there have been other moments in history that have equaled this one. Three I can readily think of are Waterloo, Watergate, and Braddock's Demise.

Annabelle rummaged through the ice packed cooler for several moments, then straightened up.

"What is it?" asked Suds, smiling down at the frowning Annabelle.

"There isn't any beer in the cooler," she explained.

"What! That's impossible!"

"No beer," said Annabelle. "Maybe in the other coolers."

"Balderdash! Zounds I say!"

Barrels pushed his hand through the ice and retrieved a six pack of Diet Pepsi. "Judas Priest! Where in the hell did this come from?" he said displaying his prize for all to see.

"Oh Boy! I love Diet Pepsi," said Annabelle.

In seconds the Fire House Five emptied the contents of all four coolers on the deck. There we six cases of assorted diet colas, a few eight-pack of vegetable juice, and a full case of Perrier water.

Suds examined a green bottle at arms-length. "That's Perrier," explained Annabelle cheerfully.

"What?"

"It's mineral water," she said.

Suds sat the bottle down and lifted his face toward the heavens.

"Great Caesar's Ghost," he muttered. "This is the unkindest cut of all."

"Is there a store where we can get some beer?" someone asked.

I explained that everything was closed on Sundays and I was sure we could borrow a six-pack or so from another boat, but that was all.

After several moments of deliberation, Hops informed me that they would not go out today and that since I had no other charter, I could keep the money.

Try as I may, I couldn't alter their decision and within a half an hour, they were packed and gone.

Annabelle sat on the port gunnel tracing the water with her toes.

"I couldn't give them back their money. They were... wonderful to let me keep it!"

I just nodded and patted her on the head.

"Do you think they'll bring their wives the next time?" she asked.

Chapter 4

~~~~~~~~

Cleveland's Tuna

He said to them,
"Children, have you caught anything to eat?"
"Not a thing." They answered.
"Cast your net off the starboard side,"
He suggested, "and you will find something."
So they made a cast, and took so many fish
They could not haul the net in.

(Saint Joseph Edition of The New American Bible, John 21:5-6)

On early winter evenings, years ago, it was often my custom to sit in my overstuffed chair before the fire and read the newspaper. I always saved the comic strip 'til last. It was my daughter, Abigail's, and her cat, Spooky's, habit to join me for a discussion of the day's events and a reading of the only sensible part of the paper. On one particular evening, Abby came trundling in wearing a long flannel nightgown with the cat draped over her shoulders.

"Hi Dad," she said, giving me that 'I got problems with my homework' look.

"What's wrong?" I asked as she deposited Spooky on the arm of the chair and plopped down in my lap.

"Miss Lockwood, my science teacher, gave us a project. I have to do one on fish because you're a fisherman," sighed Abby.

"And you need my help, right?" I asked.

"Would you?" asked Abby.

"I suppose so," I said, "But I'll only show you how to get the answers you need. Is that fair enough?"

Abby pulled her nightgown tight around her toes. "What's the biggest fish you ever got, Dad?"

"Ah ha, my little chickadee," I said in my best **W. C. Fields** voice. "The biggest fish I ever got was a giant hogapotamus fish."

"The what?" asked Abby, confused.

"Ah, yes. The giant hogapotamus fish. Haven't you heard of him?" I continued to tease.

Abby grinned and gave me her 'oh no, here we go again' stare. "There's no such thing, Dad."

"Why yes, my dear. They're so big they nibble on old railroad cars and swallow ships. And I know for a fact that some are swimming down off Bermuda disguised as triangles doing all sorts of naughty things."

Abby snuggled up close and looked up at me. "I don't think you'll ever grow up, Dad."

Abigail is a young woman now, but the question hasn't changed. There isn't a week during the season that someone doesn't ask me about my biggest fish, and so far, the answer hasn't changed. It's still a giant Bluefin Tuna.

Of all the game fish in all the seas of the world, there is nothing quite like this giant blue fish. Only the great black marlin off the coast of Australia may be his equal, but that hasn't been definitively proven yet. Rod and reel has landed black marlin in the 1,500-pound range, but no one on earth, at least as of this writing, have taken a bluefin over 1,496 pounds — not because a fish of that size doesn't exist, but no one's been able to hang onto one of these beasts. The black marlin gives a spectacular running, jumping, dogging battle that's a wonderful sight to behold, whereas the bluefin depends on speed. They have been clocked at 60 miles per hour, an unimaginably awesome power. All one has to do is take a close look at this fish to see that when God designed him, he had his evolution department working overtime. The fish is fluid, dynamically perfect in shape. His pectoral and dorsal fins fold back into clefts in his body so there is no drag. His crescent-shaped tail is driven by an engine-like backbone that's powered by an oversized heart. The outer skin, for lack of another word, is nothing but slick, blue-steel armor plates that are so tough packing houses use chain saws when dressing the fish.

A noted fresh water angler of some renown, asked one of my fellow captains, Captain Magpie, what it was like to fight a tuna.

The captain said, "Well, just figure something weighing almost half a ton going 50 miles an hour away from you, and you're tied to it on a line and have got to stop it."

The man looked at the huge rods and reels in Captain Magpie's cockpit and shrugged his shoulders and walked away. "No sir'ree. That's not my sport," he said.

A hooked or harpooned tuna is an unpredictable, highly dangerous fish that if not handled properly can create mayhem. Woe to the angler who thinks he can overpower one of these beasts. Usually, all he gets for his trouble are bruised or broken ribs and a parted line.

I remember a certain linebacker from a pro football team that had to sit out for three weeks while his cracked ribs healed after fighting a tuna at sea. And on one occasion I was almost killed by a spent fish that had been fought, gaffed, and unhooked. I was leading this dead fish to the stern cleat by a tail strap and safety rope when he lunged, tearing the flying gaff out of him, throwing me to the deck, and swimming off with 100 feet of three-quarter inch polypropylene rope wrapped around his tail. Had I not been able to let go of that rope, it would have been all over.

I have seen tuna close to 800 pounds boated in less than one hour and numerous times I've seen fish weighing 500 pounds taking five or six hours to bring to gaff. I know of one battle that lasted over 10 hours, and the fish was only a little guy around 400 pounds.

Tuna fishing, like yacht racing or baseball, is a team sport, where success is dependent on the combined effort of the team, as well as the skill of the individual. Even when everyone is performing up to par, there's still a 50 percent chance that a hooked or harpooned fish will get away.

Up until the early 1970s, tuna fish were worth very little money in this country. Most fishermen who went after them either released the fish or sold it to a local packer for a few cents a pound. This came to an abrupt halt one day when a group of Japanese businessmen visited a local fish dealer and saw several 500-pound fish being carted off to the cat food factory. Their remarks and actions from that day forward loosely translated into something like, "Stupid children threw gift away and play with wrapper, [and] hey gang, I bet we can have these suckers for a song." What we once sold for pet food or discarded was one of the most highly regarded foods of the Japanese people. The same tuna that is $50 per pound in Japan sells for only $5 per pound in the states. As a result, many Japanese businessmen began buying all their tuna here.

During one week in August of 1976, four tunas were boated on the Seawitch. The first weighed 780 pounds, the second weighed 820 pounds, and the third weighed 860 pounds. The last, and the biggest, is the fish this story is about; the one I'll always remember as Cleveland's Tuna.

The best weather conditions for harpooning tuna is no condition at all. A vacant sky day and a silk flat sea with a trace of a breeze are ideal. And this particular August day dawned perfect, with a hot red sun that shot straight up from the horizon towing the temperature with it. By 9:30 a.m., it was over 80 degrees Fahrenheit and still climbing. Our charter for the day, for one reason or another, had postponed their blue fishing trip, and Cleveland and I found ourselves with our first day off in over three weeks.

"I'm glad they called last night," she said, digging into a platter of pancakes. "It was nice to sleep in a bit. I feel wonderful."

"Well, what would you like to do today?" I asked, as the Captain of the Indian and the Captain of the 'Magpie' joined us at our table.

"Morning sweetheart," said Captain Magpie, giving Cleveland a peck on the cheek. "How're the pancakes?"

"Great. Are you guys going in?" asked Cleveland.

"No trip," said Captain Indian. "I sent mine home and Captain Magpie's got an afternoon sight-seeing trip."

Captain Magpie stared at his friend across the table. "Now Captain, why don't you tell 'em what happened this morning."

Captain Indian's face went blank. "Nothing really. I was warming the engine up, and I went over to the yard to get ice. When I got back, my mate had the party aboard, and we were ready to go. I put the ice aboard and this guy, who booked the trip, tells me I'm five minutes late. He doesn't want to pay me by the trip, but by the hour. I told him he paid for eight hours and he would get eight hours because I would give him any lost time at the end of the trip. Well, he said he was going to keep track of every hour and that he was going to make sure he got his money's worth. So, I just reached over and turned the engine off and handed him his deposit back. I told him I wouldn't feel comfortable with him on my boat and I left."

"And that's it, you just walked off?" asked Cleveland.

"That's right. He came running after me and I send him over to the 'Redfin,' but he didn't stay long. Captain Smith threw him off his boat."

"Why?"

"I'll tell you why," interrupted Captain Magpie. "Smith had that bastard out last year. His mate cleaned and packed four Blue Fish for that guy, and he gave the girl a $2 tip. Smith was **rip shit** cause his mate didn't tell him until after the guy left."

Cleveland looked around the table. "I had a lot of trouble my first two years, but it wasn't because people were cheap. It was because a lot of men resented a woman working on a boat. I guess they felt their private world was being invaded or something."

Captain Magpie gazed at Cleveland. "You can invade my world anytime, green eyes."

"Oh gosh, Captain Magpie. If... if only... "

"If only what, beautiful?"

"If only you weren't married and so damn repulsive."

"Well, you can't have everything," laughed Captain Magpie.

"Oh yes I can," said Cleveland, "But you haven't got anything I want."

"Women just don't understand me. See what happens. You give them a compliment and you get shot down."

Cleveland stretched over and gave Captain Magpie a kiss on his forehead. "If you weren't so lovable, you'd be dangerous," she said.

Captain Indian looked at his watch and checked it with one over the counter. "Let's get going. It's too damn nice to sit on the beach. I got a good feeling I'm going to stick one today."

"You're not coming out?" asked Captain Magpie.

"No, we've had a good week with three fish, and we haven't had a day off in ages. Besides I think Cleveland may have plans of her own."

Cleveland was mouthing, "No way in hell do I want to stay ashore today" when Captain Magpie handed her a piece of yellow paper.

"Is this true?" she asked, reading the paper and handing it to me.

"Sure," said Captain Indian. "I got that price on the phone 20 minutes ago. Change your mind, Capt.?"

"I believe so," I said, watching my mate nod approval.

Cleveland ran the boat down the channel just above trolling speed, while I carefully laid 600 feet of white 600-pound test braided nylon line into a plastic milk crate that we used as a line basket. Each foot of line had to be visually checked for cuts, broken strands, and knots. One end of the line held a snap that was connected to a fluorescent orange tuna ball. This is a tear drop-shaped heavy rubber buoy that's 30 inches in diameter, and the other or business end of the line is connected to a brass dart or lily. In rigging, one had to be certain that everything is in its proper place and that nothing will foul a harpoon or line when it's thrown. A loose coil or an improperly positioned line can cause damage, lose a fish, or kill a man.

A harpoon is made of three components: a 12- to 14-foot wood or aluminum pole, a brass socket, and an 18- to 20-inch black iron shaft that's beveled at its tip to fit a slot beneath the flukes of the dart. The line from the dart is held along the length of the pole by small strips of masking or electrician's tape. When in position, 25 to 30 feet of line is loosely coiled in a throwing bucket, which is hung under the lip of the pulpit. The line from the throwing bucket to the line basket is held in position by clothespins along the entire pulpit back to the basket.

Once a harpoon is thrown, nothing holds it to the boat except a few clothespins that will snap free as a stricken fish dives. When everything works perfectly, and this isn't always the case, line spills free from the throwing basket as the harpoon leaves the hand. The fish is stuck, and the dart is driven deep into the body. As the fish dives, the water pressure pulls the shaft free of the dart. The tape strips that hold the line to the pole are broken, and the pole and shaft float free, leaving the dart and line in the fish. They are picked up after fish, line, and ball are clear of the boat. As the fish runs, the line is snapped free of the clothespins and all 600 feet of line is pulled from the basket into the water, followed by the tuna ball. All this happens in about 12 seconds, and heaven help the person who, for one reason or another, got a foot or hand tangled in the line. I believe I've set track records getting off the pulpit once I knew the dart was driven home.

Boat handling during this type of tuna fishing or with rod and reel requires a professional at the wheel, and I believe no one could do the job any better than Cleveland. Although we didn't fish tuna as a steady diet, Cleveland was good as they come when it comes to maneuvering, positioning, and stalking a pushing tuna. She had developed a feel for the boat and its controls and could make it perform exactly as she wished.

Slipping up over the back of a surface cruising tuna fish wasn't always an easy job, as it doesn't take much to spook a fish, or on occasion, overrun one. The wrong turn, too much or too little power would have you looking at a spent wake and rising bubbles.

Captain Indian came abreast of us in the channel and pulled back his power as he pointed toward the west. Cleveland waved and turned into his wake as he again resumed speed.

"You ready yet?" she called over the windshield.

I dropped down on one knee as the Seawitch lifted up and over the Indians' wake. "Go ahead," I yelled over the sound of the departing diesel.

Cleveland applied power evenly, lifting our bow clear and matching the Indian's speed. In a few minutes we were past the bell and turned toward the northwest. Cleveland switched on the digital fathometer, watched it warm up, then told Angel Base that we and the Indian were out sticking for the day and that we would be standing by on the CB tuna channel.

I busied myself tying a rolled red fighting flag to our starboard outrigger and cleared the cockpit of anything that might get in the way.

Something dappled and glittered on the surface a half-mile off our port bow. I whistled and pointed as Cleveland quickly swung the pulpit directly at the disturbance and glanced through her binoculars.

"Blue fish," she said turning back on course. "I'm going to start looking when we hit 70 feet, okay?"

I nodded and pointed along a line of drifting clumps of marsh grass that had ebbed out with the dropping tide. "Careful," I remarked, remembering that we had almost collided with a partially submerged log floating in the grass the previous day.

"You were at the wheel, not me, Captain. It wasn't that I was distracted by that ... that woman."

"Now just you wait a minute," I said tying to defend myself. "Just be—"

"Just, just what?" Cleveland interrupted. "Just because she's a famous English actress and does all those epics on the BBC and gets introduced by Alice the cook every week? Or was it just because she had on a bikini that was just two strings and a promise? Just what was it?"

"Allister," I said. "Not Alice."

"Don't change the subject, Captain. That's what all the kids at school call him. Don't tell me that you weren't just a teeny-weeny little bit taken with her," continued Cleveland.

"More startled and embarrassed than anything else," I admitted.

Cleveland tilted her head back and fluttered her eye lashes. "Oh, Captain! You wouldn't mind if I took the sun in the nude, would you?" she said in a British accent.

"Good grief! I'm doomed. You're never going to let me forget that little scene, are you?"

Cleveland doubled over in laughter. "You should have seen your face. Thank God her husband put his foot down or you would have had to watch her big white rump riding up and down on the bow all afternoon."

I shook my head. "You know, actually, they were real nice people. You wouldn't believe they've been married 18 years, would you? They behaved like a couple of kids on their honeymoon."

"That's because they're still in love. I could see that the minute they came on the boat," added Cleveland. "She's a little uninhibited, and maybe that's one of the reasons he loves her."

"I suppose so, but I'll be honest with you. I was damn glad she put some clothes on," I added. "68 feet, I'm going to slow down."

I took a pair of binoculars and stood on the life jacket box as Cleveland busied herself with the controls. Even through my dark sunglasses it was impossible to keep from squinting in the almost 100-degree temperature. The sea mirrored and shimmered like unwrinkled tin foil on all points of the compass, and every dark painted surface on the boat turned blistering hot to the touch. Had it not been for the lack of humidity, it would have been unbearable. The sun reached for its zenith while mirages of strange land masses and dark green islands floated just above the far horizon on silver rivers of heat.

"You know, we don't have to be out," I said after a time. "We can go back if you like. Money isn't everything."

"It is when you're in college," Cleveland flatly replied. "Besides, how many days do we get to go sticking? And who knows how long that price will hold?"

"You're right, I suppose, but you seem to be becoming a little mercenary all of the sudden."

Cleveland's face showed hurt. "That's not it at all, Capt. I don't think you understand my feelings."

"I'm sorry, you want to explain?"

"How many days have I missed in four summers?"

"I can't think of any," I said.

"Well, you know, this may be my last year Capt., and I want to spend every good day I can on the water. I'm not sure I'm coming back next year."

"Why not?" I asked.

"Oh, my folks think I should be doing something with my education, and they want me to start thinking about the future. They said I can't work on a boat forever, so just like in the beer commercial, I'm trying to grab all the gusto I can because I'm not sure just how long I've got left. You understand?" she asked, looking for approval.

"Sure, but you've got the rest of the summer and all of next season if you want. I wouldn't be sad about leaving just yet. I mean, after all where in the hell are you going to find a job that gets you up at four in the morning, works you 14 hours a day, and pays you peanuts?" I added.

Cleveland thought for a moment, then burst out laughing. "Just like an elephant, right Capt.?"

"That's right," I said. "Don't worry, this boat will always be here whenever you want it, and you can always come and fish."

"I know," she said, "But somehow things are never the same when you try to go back. Everything changes. I went back to Shaker Heights for Christmas vacation, and I got together with some of my old high school friends. It was fun, but everyone was different; everything had changed."

"This won't," I said. "People change, but this won't."

Cleveland lifted her sunglasses and blinked in the brilliant light. "What do you mean, Capt.? Everything changes."

"Not this," I began. "People and the times change, but the sea and its mystery and adventure are always with us. Even when we're old and can't deal in it, it's still here offering the same things to us as when we first found it. It was here before us and it will be here long after we're gone. And even if we have to leave it for a time, it's always waiting for us when we return."

Cleveland said nothing for a long moment. "Oh, I guess it's just me," she admitted. "I don't want to leave it for a minute. It's just selfish, I guess."

"I know how you feel," I told her. "I'd feel the same if I thought I had to give it up and do something else. However, I wouldn't worry because you never know how things are going to turn out."

Cleveland lifted her sunglasses again and grinned. "Oh really, my dear Captain?" she said in her British accent. "One doesn't always know what one will do, does one?"

"I'd kind of like to forget that, if you don't mind," I murmured turning away from her teasing.

The Indian pointed toward us for a moment, then cut his bow sharply back to the northwest as I went reaching for my binoculars.

"Just ahead of him," I heard Cleveland say as she altered our direction to a point a half mile in front of the Indian.

At first, all I could see was ribbons of heat shimmering on the empty plane, but then several sickle-shaped spikes cut the water and disappeared.

"Those are his fish," said Cleveland. "I don't want to get too close. Let's see what they do."

I was watching Captain Indian trade places with his mate, then run for the pulpit when our bow swung sharply away to the north.

"Oh boy!" said Cleveland to herself as our diesel took on a different sound.

"What are you looking at?" I shouted down to her.

Cleveland was now standing on the seat steering the boat with her bare feet. "You better get up front. They'll show again. Just keep looking ahead."

I stepped over the engine box and grabbed the bow rail just as three sets of tail and dorsal fins sliced the water less than 200 yards in the distance. They turned a little to the east and swam in a perfect line abreast, leaving a three-V wake spilling behind them on the undisturbed sea. From now on, any communication between Cleveland and I would be in the form of hand signals.

I untied the four safety straps that lashed the harpoon to the pulpit, then kicked out of my deck shoes and waited as the three fish showed no signs of changing course or speed.

Captain Indian was out on his pulpit holding a raised harpoon while several pods of tuna skirted his bow and crisscrossed ahead. It looked like he was herding them with a 14-foot cattle prod.

Our diesel changed to a lower pitch as we came within 100 yards of the fish. Cleveland knew from experience that it would be best to follow them for a while, letting them get used to the sound of the engine and that a slow gradual approach on these newly surfaced fish would be our only chance for a shot. There had been times when we would rush right in when the circumstances permitted and throw, but this was usually on overcast days and on pods of milling fish.

I didn't see Captain Indian throw, but when I looked in his direction a ball was passing his **stern**, and he was turning to the west. Cleveland gave me a thumbs-up signal and pointed at the ball that was now skidding toward the southwest, kicking up a lot of spray. Well, that's half the battle, I thought. Now the fun begins.

Our pod stayed up and on course for another five minutes, letting us close the distance to less than 200 feet. I now was able to see their dark shapes below the fins and this was the first inkling I had of their size. These were big fish, but how big only God knew at this point. I was watching their crescent-shaped tails swing effortlessly from side to side when for no apparent reason, they slipped below the surface and were gone. Cleveland stayed on course a few more seconds, then shifted into neutral, and we slowly lost headway.

"I don't think I was close enough to spook 'em," she said over the windshield. "I'm sure they'll come up again."

I shrugged my shoulders and sat down on the hatch cover. "You didn't spook them. They just took a powder. How's Indian doing?"

Cleveland ducked down and spent a minute on the radio, while I squinted at the glaring empty sea.

"He lost the fish!" she exclaimed standing back up on the helmsman seat. "He said the fish pulled the dart. He's coming back this way."

"Did you tell him ours went down?" I asked.

"Yep, I told him to keep his eyes open. Boy! I was sure we were going to get a shot at them. They looked huge!" exclaimed Cleveland.

"You better believe it," I said. "Maybe if we're lucky they might show again."

Several minutes passed, and I started to grow impatient. "Perhaps we ought to start trolling in a wide circle," I suggested. "Those weren't the only tuna out here.

Cleveland did a slow 360 on the **helmsman seat**. "Let's wait a couple of more seconds. I thought I smelled something, and I got that feeling."

That was all I needed. No way was I going to go against Cleveland's famous nose or her intuition. Four years of working with Cleveland, this redheaded Polish girl from Shaker Heights, had prepared me to sit out here in this heat until the sea boiled away or hell froze over. No matter what, when Cleveland said 'stay', the Seawitch stayed.

The Indian materialized several thousand yards off our port and was almost past us when our transmission slipped into gear.

"What did I tell you? There they are!" Cleveland said pointing back over our stern.

Oh, Lord! I thought, how does she do it? As I watched the fins sway through the calm water 200 yards away.

Cleveland spun the Seawitch around on her axis and chose a course that would intercept the pod. "I'm going to go straight in. We may get a shot before they dive. OK?"

I nodded agreement and headed for the pulpit, checking the clothespins and coil of line in the throwing basket. At our present speed and heading, I would be over the fish in less than two minutes, providing they didn't alter course or sink out of sight. Forty yards from the pod, Cleveland cut back across their wake and then adding power, turned directly into it. The huge black shapes were now less than 25 yards from the tip of my harpoon. The last few feet seemed like eternity as visions of my boyhood hunts with my father and uncles in South Carolina came to mind.

"Remember Bobby, if you're going to hunt God's creatures, you got to aim true. Anything else is a disgrace and a sin before the Lord." I lifted the harpoon and pointed it at the middle fish while the shapes took on clarity and distinction as the distance fell away. 'Lord Jesus,' I prayed, 'guide my hand' as I reared back and pushed the harpoon with every ounce of strength I could muster from my 6-foot, 220-pound frame.

The two tuna on the outside of the middle fish were sinking and my target appeared to be rising as the arching harpoon slammed into the socket in the great fish's back. In an instant, the tuna rolled on his side, showing his tremendous white belly, then dove, tearing the line from the clothespins and basket, warping it away at incredible speed. Cleveland had thrown the Seawitch into reverse the second the harpoon left my hand and swung the bow away from the diving fish. I could do nothing but watch as the last 200 feet of line disappeared over the side, pulling the ball after it.

Cleveland watched the ball pull away in a cloud of spray, then shouted that he was the biggest tuna that she'd ever seen.

I said nothing for a moment and sat down on the hatch cover, rubbing my aching right shoulder. I couldn't recall ever having thrown anything so hard in my life. "I think I **smote** him a mighty blow," I finally said, grinning up at Cleveland.

"Damn straight. You nailed him beautifully, but I don't see the harpoon. It hasn't popped up yet."

The fluorescent ball was now a quarter mile from us and heading toward the northeast.

"There it is, I pointed as the pole bobbed up and down 50 yards from us.

Cleveland put us in gear, and in a few minutes, we were examining the shaft that was bent 90 degrees from the socket. I doubted it could ever be straightened, but we had extras, and they were expendable anyway. After a 10-minute steam at full throttle, we caught up with our ball, then dropped back 100 yards and matched its speed, which was about 5 miles an hour.

Our usual procedure was to follow the ball for one hour, then add an extra ball to the line to increase drag, then follow him till the fish died. After that, it would be a simple matter of hauling the fish in, gaffing it, tying it alongside, and towing it home. What we didn't know at the time was that this fish didn't know or give a damn about our procedures, as he had a mind of his own.

Cleveland unfurled our fighting flag and ran it up the outrigger as I un-coiled our flying gaff and laced its 20-foot rope to the **starboard cleat.** I positioned an empty line basket amid ship, so the 600 feet could be coiled in as the fish was hauled in. Tail straps and tow lines were laid out on the engine box. The spare harpoon was rigged, and a fresh basket of line was place on the bow, as it was not uncommon to take a second fish while wait-ing for the first fish to die.

Captain Indian and Angel Base called Cleveland and wished us luck, as well as Captain Magpie. He had just cleared the channel with a party of white-haired ladies from the Daughters of the American Revolution.

Meanwhile, our fish never altered course or speed. If everything remained constant, he would be off Race Point in four hours. Cleveland watched the fluorescent buoy V the water for a long time.

"Do you suppose he's in pain?" she said eventually.

"Fish don't feel pain like we do," I answered. "They have a different nervous system. What makes you ask?"

"Oh, I don't know. It's just that before I came to work for you, I couldn't kill a fly or step on a bug. And now all I've been doing this week is helping kill these huge beautiful things. And somehow, I don't understand why I love it so much. It really isn't the money."

"You asking me for answers or a justification?"

"Both, I guess. Sometimes it's hard to understand your own feelings about things," Cleveland said, seemingly confused.

"You know what Hemingway said about it, don't you?"

"No, I don't. What did he say?"

"He said don't try to understand it or analyze it because you'll just get confused."

"Is that how you feel, Capt.?"

"I feel that fish will feed 1,000 people and provide employment for a few dozen more, beginning with us. As far as enjoying it, well, I think those feelings go way back to when we were living out of caves and clubbing mastodons. The guy who clubbed the most, ate the most. It wasn't the killing he enjoyed. It was knowing that if he did a good job he and his family would eat."

"You mean I enjoy this because my grandfathers clubbed dinosaurs?"

"Yes ma'am. It goes all the way back to when Eve got herself and Adam kicked out of the garden over that apple business. See what you women got started? Why, we wouldn't have to be out here under this boiling sun chasing that poor innocent fish if it hadn't been for the likes of you."

Cleveland pointed at the spare harpoon and suggested that I take a little swim in front of the pulpit as my brain was starting to bake in the sun. "Go on," she said smiling sweetly. "It will be nice and cool."

One hour and five minutes had elapsed since striking the fish, and he hadn't shown the first sign of tiring, and his direction hadn't varied 10 degrees. I readied a second ball as Cleveland pulled alongside the first. Using a bass gaff, I reefed in the line and snapped a swivel around it, then dropped both balls back into the water. Cleveland kept the speed of the boat with the fish for a moment, then dropped back to the 100-yard interval.

"That ought to do it," I said. "We'll pull him in an hour, that is if he hasn't died first."

Cleveland checked the tachometer and looked at the balls pulling ahead of us. "He hasn't slowed a bit," she announced. "I got a good look at him when he was diving, and he's huge. It might take us longer."

600 feet of half inch line and two 30-inch balls would create a tremendous drag and I doubted this tuna would be able to keep up such a high speed and pull that load much longer. After all, we had taken the last three fish in less than two and a half hours, and even though this one appeared larger, I doubted that it would take that much more.

One hour and 50 minutes later, the balls stopped pulling and bobbed upright for the first time. We were somewhere near the center of the bay in 20 fathoms of water, and we were over 14 miles from where we had first harpooned the fish.

Cleveland eased up to the balls, and I was about to reach for the line when she threw the throttle into full, knocking me backwards and turning the Seawitch sharply to port. I stumbled to my feet just in time to see a mound of pushing water followed by two fins and our line passed our stern heading southeast. We stood speechless as the balls pulled halfway under, then skipped off over the surface, kicking spray.

"Just like the shark movie, isn't it?" she remarked.

I just shook my head and thought that God hadn't made a shark that could keep up with a bluefin tuna. "Nice job," I said. "If you hadn't seen him we would have run over the line and cut him off."

"He was just changing direction. That's why the balls stopped moving, but I can't understand why he came to the surface."

"Maybe he wanted to see what we looked like."

"I guess so," Cleveland said catching my eyes. "I suppose we at least owe him that, only I wish we could kill him quick. Is there some way we can do it?"

There is," I explained, "But there's a good chance he'll pull the dart, and we could lose him. It's a go-for-broke deal; an all-or-nothing thing, and he's worth a lot of money to us."

"We'll get him if we let the gear kill him. I mean we won't lose him now, will we? It will just take time until he dies. Like the others, right?"

"That's right," I answered, watching her carefully. "Just like the others, only I don't know how long this fish will take."

Cleveland turned and followed the departing buoys with her sea-green eyes, then turned back to the helm and me.

"It's up to you," I said.

A strange smile filled Cleveland's lovely face. "What was that you said? Go for broke?"

"That's right," I laughed. "Why the hell not. Like you said, maybe we owe this one."

"OK. Great, but what do we do?" she inquired.

"Just catch up to the balls like before and pull alongside, then do exactly as I tell you. It will be easier to explain it as we go along."

Cleveland dropped the transmission into gear again and brought the throttle forward to a slow cruise. In 10 minutes we were with the two balls, matching their speed. "Now what?" she questioned.

I checked the direction the fish was heading, then went aft and switched the gaff line from starboard to port. "Pull alongside," I ordered.

"My God! You're going to let him pull the boat?" Cleveland called.

"That's right. If the dart doesn't pull and the line holds, this 8 tons of fiberglass will kill him quick."

Cleveland's lower jaw went slack for an instant.

"You're having second thoughts?" I asked.

"Hell no! I'm just getting used to the idea. I never thought we'd use this boat for a cork. I used to fish with a cork on a line when we lived in Solen, a suburb of Cleveland."

"You got it," I said. "Now, when I lift these buoys aboard, I'm going to hold the line up, and you just keep the boat pointed along the line. When I tell you, start reducing headway a little at a time, letting the fish take up the slack."

Cleveland cut in tight, and I dropped both balls on the engine box and held the line waist-high for a moment, feeling the powerful undulations of the fish before passing it around the starboard cleat.

"Start bringing your power back, real slow," I said. In a few seconds the sound of the engine dulled, and the line stretched, pulling our stern to starboard. "That's it. Now go into neutral."

Cleveland pushed the lever upright, and the stern swung around to face the fish. "My God! He's towing us. I can't believe it!"

"That's right," I said, walking forward and turning the engine off. "And he hasn't pulled the dart. We just may get him."

Cleveland looked over the stern and watched the water hump us and push to the side, forming a wake. "How long do you suppose this will take? I mean, he can't keep this up for too long, can he?"

Heaven only knows, I thought.

I looked at my watch and sat down beside Cleveland. "Do you want to tell me about Solen? You said you used to fish there?"

"Yeah, it was great. We had this little pond near the house, and I loved fishing there. I made hooks out of pins and once in a while I got a fish, but when we moved to Shaker Heights I couldn't fish anymore," she murmured.

"Did you miss Solen?"

"I guess so," she sighed.

Cleveland skipped on to the next topic. "Did I ever tell you that we had this river in Cleveland that was so polluted that it used to catch on fire?"

"Was it any hotter than this?" I asked, pointing at the shimmering heat rising along the horizon.

"I'm not sure," she laughed, "but this sure smells better. I hope he dies soon. God, I hope this fish dies quick. He's nothing like the others, is he?"

"Only bigger, that's all."

"How old do you think he is?"

"Maybe as old as you. I don't know," I said unsure.

"I've killed thousands of fish in the last four years, and I always felt it was a necessary thing. I love fishing, but this fish. He's different. He's nothing like we've ever had on before, is he? I mean, he's like the last of something and we're killing him." she questioned.

"He's not the last. And no fish dies of old age," I said. "There are things in this pond besides us that feed on his kind."

"What?"

"Killer whales. I've seen them kill tuna by the hundreds off Provincetown." I explained.

"They do it because they're hungry. We're doing it for money. And some people do it for fun."

I took Cleveland's chin in my hand and turned her face toward me. "There are different kinds of hunger," I explained. "People feed different ways. Understand?"

Cleveland faced away, looking toward the fish. "I was starting to hate him because he was making me feel guilty. I love him and hate him. You follow me?"

"I think respect is about all we can afford," I said. "That fish is doing his job, and we're doing ours. That's what God put him in the sea for. He's food for us and other creatures."

Cleveland reached down and felt the taut line. "Well, we gave him a chance, and we're going our best, aren't we? We can be proud of that, I guess."

"That's right," I said checking my watch. "He's been towing us 20 minutes. I don't think it will take much longer."

45 minutes into the tow and a little less than four hours after striking the bluefin, the line stopped moving and went slack. Our fish lay dead on the bottom in 15 fathoms of water and over 17 miles from where we had first seen him.

Captain Bill of the 'Night Mender' was in the immediate area and radioed to offer assistance, which we gratefully accepted. Lifting an average tuna 90 feet to the surface was not an easy job. Lifting this tuna was torture. We pulled, sweated, cursed, and strained under the scorching sun for every foot of line. Bill gritted his teeth and swore that we had shafted a whale and was gonna call the fish police as soon as we got the son of a bitch up.

However, we all went silent and forgot our pain as the water beneath the Seawitch turned a dull pearl shade. At 30 feet, the tuna's white belly seemed to fill the sea. We held our silence as the last few feet of line came over the gunnel and the enormous fish at last broke the surface. Bill and Cleveland held on as I hit the fish with the flying gaff. Cleveland then slipped a loop over the tail, and it was all over.

Bill reached out and gave Cleveland a hug, shook my hand, and stared at the fish. "He's 12 feet long," he said. "Let me know what he weighs in at."

Cleveland looked up and down the length and girth of the bluefin. "Oh my gosh!" was all she could manage at the time.

I untied the 'Night Mender' as Bill pushed off. It was a long, quiet ride home that day. Cleveland fought a battle with a great fish and a greater battle within herself. Reason, compassion, logic, respect, and understanding had played a part — had skirmished and triumphed over again.

She had flung the dice, letting compassion and respect carry her through and with them we had won it all.

The fish was trucked to a Sandwich fish buyer that night, who found it too large for his scales. The head was removed, and the two pieces were weighed individually. The total weight was 1,340 pounds, making it one of the largest tuna fish ever taken with a harpoon in the world at the time.

Chapter 5

The Blitz

It is a well-established scientific fact that the striped bass is one of the most intelligent of fishes, and it is also well noted by sportsmen that this fish is very selective in its choice of food. There is a continuing challenge to find out what they will eat at a given time on a given day. To say that they're picky or finicky is a gross understatement. Stripers have been known to make fishermen and charter boat captains cry. I have seen bass swim through a school of plump mackerel with their noses turned up and feed on dime-size grass shrimp instead. Other times they will take blueback herring and not touch blackback flounder. Sometimes only the most delicate shade of color on a plug or gig will entice them. And there are times when, for days on end, they will lay on the bottom and sulk. I would be correct in saying that most of the time, they behave in a perfectly disrespectful way toward man.

However, dear friends, they do have a weakness, a sort of chink in their armor that causes them to throw all caution to the wind and behave like children on Christmas morning. This weakness is squid. Striped bass welcome squid the same way the seventh fleet would welcome the Rockettes.

When all the conditions are right, and the factors come together, stripers will turn the sea for miles around into a battleground. I have experienced feeding frenzies or blitzes that lasted from six hours to three days. One of the most memorable ones in my career to date occurred while our nation was preparing to celebrate its 200th birthday.

Thursday, July 1, 1976, 8:30 a.m.

Cleveland and I began this morning thinking that this would be an easy trip. Not only was the weather perfect, we had one of our best crews of fishermen aboard. They were experts with the tackle and all could do my job as well as hers. This was always a treat for us because it was nice to step back and be passengers on your boat and get paid for it.

However, fate and nature had a few surprises in store for us. We had just passed the No. 1 navigation buoy about six miles northeast of Barnstable, when all the ingredients for the drama ahead started to fall into place.

"How many boats going to be out here today, Capt.?" asked John Mortimer, a dark-haired car dealer from Brockton.

Jack Dillon, a plastic manufacturer from the same town, squinted behind his sunglasses and started pointing with his finger. "Hell, I just counted 50, and I bet before noon there'll be 200 or so."

"Good heavens! I bet there will be 500 out here on the Fourth," someone else added.

Captain Magpie was in the process of telling Angel Base just how much alcohol Captain Lobster had consumed at the last July Fourth party, when Captain Lobster came on the air.

Captain Lobster, in a soft friendly voice: *Switch over.*

Every charter boat that was listening turned their CBs to channel 11 and waited.

Captain Lobster: *You guys on here?*

I keyed my mic and let him know I was on.

Captain Lobster: *Where's Magpie? I haven't got all damn day!*

Captain Magpie: *I'm waiting. What have you got?*

Captain Lobster: *I've got a mild indication.*

Seawitch: *Yeah, what is it?*

Captain Lobster: *Well I'm only going to say it one time, so you guys get it straight cause I ain't gonna repeat it.*

Captain Magpie: *OK, what have you got?*

Captain Lobster, in a quiet voice: *I just saw squid.*

The radio went stone silent for a moment.

Captain Magpie answered quickly: *Thank you.*

My crew had been listening and now began double-checking everything. However, Cleveland hadn't heard because she was below changing out of her combat uniform of faded cutoffs, t-shirt, and top siders into a new green bikini, complete with baseball hat, oversized sunglasses, and layers of some kind of lard substance that for all the world looked like she had applied it to her nose with a putty knife.

"What's all the fuss? I didn't hear," she said, stepping from the cabin.

"You planning on sunbathing today?" asked the plastic manufacturer obviously delighted with Cleveland's new costume.

"Sure thing. I'm going up on the bow, and you guys call me if you need me, OK?

"Well, someone just spotted squid," I said.

Cleveland took off her sunglasses and looked in my direction. "Yeah?" she said.

"Yeah," I repeated.

"Oh boy," she squealed, ducking back in the cabin. "I'll be right out."

Three-quarters of a mile to our west, the 'Lobster' sat almost motionless in the flat sea while the Indian and the 'Magpie' vessels crisscrossed his stern at a slow speed.

> Captain Lobster: *Why don't you set out, Seawitch, and work this way? We ain't seen nothing yet.*

I eased the throttle back to trolling speed and turned to the west.

John Mortimer turned in the fish finder as we slowed down and gazed intently at the matching while the stylus drew a slow curving line that represented the ocean floor a little less than 10 fathoms below.

"I'd like to get a load today," he said not looking away from the machine. "I told the sisters at the kids' school that I would bring them fish, and they said it would be wonderful if we got enough for them as well as some for the old folks in a rest home that their order looks after."

"Sure," I said. "Let's put out all the guns. May as well go for broke."

Cleveland came back on deck, re-suited for battle and carrying an arm full of spinning rods. "I better **rig** these," she said. "I think we're going to need them."

Within a few minutes a full complement of five trolling rods were set out, three of which pulled bar rigs, each trailing three bright red and orange squid-like hoochies on wire lines. These were adjusted to run 12 feet below the surface in an inverted V pattern. Two other rods with monofilament line were set in outriggers and each carried two hoochies in tandem that knifed the surface 50 feet behind the submerged inverted V. In all, 13 hoochies formed a small artificial school that always proved to be deadly effective when squid were around. Four spinning rods with surface popping plugs were set in ready racks. They would be used when we were stopped and trolled fish were being fought. Several needle-sharp gaff hooks laid out on the port, stern, and starboard gunwales for quick use. Boxes of spare supplies were brought up from below, along with spare rods. In a blitz there would be no time to repair anything if it malfunctioned or broke. It would be tossed below and taken care of later. Pliers, knives, and gloves were passed out and two five-gallon plastic buckets were filled with sea water so that we could wash the blood off the deck and our hands quickly.

With inexperienced fishermen, the mate and myself would spend our time navigating, setting out lines, gaffing, unhooking fish, and instructing. However, with this crew, we would become two more members of a well-trained team on a very efficient fishing machine.

9:00 a.m.

Cleveland took her post atop the life jacket box and peered over the windshield through binoculars, while the rest of us scanned the horizon in every direction for a sign. Several outboards sped by, then slowed and started working back toward us.

First outboard: *You get anything, Magpie?*

Captain Magpie: *No. I haven't seen anything all morning.*

Second outboard: *Then why are you guys all fishing here? Ain't anyone got any?*

Seawitch: *No, not that I know of, but you can't trust the rest of these* **Barnstable Harbor** *boats. They wouldn't tell if they did anyway. You wouldn't either, Magpie. You're just as bad as the rest.*

Captain Magpie: *I am, am I? When did you ever call me in on fish?*

Third outboard: *Well never, but I would call you today if I found them.*

Seawitch: *OK, you call me first. And if I get a fish, I'll call you back, but don't tell the rest of these guys, OK? Yeah Magpie. I won't tell anybody but you. The rest of your Barnstable guys better not listen when I call, Magpie.*

Captain Indian: *Don't worry. We won't listen. We promise.*

9:15 a.m.

"Watermelon! I smell watermelon!" shouted Cleveland standing on her tip toes, pushing her head higher over the windshield.

No one said anything, but everyone sniffed the sea air as the faint, but unmistakable smell of fresh-cut watermelon filled the cockpit. People unaccustomed to sport fishing at sea are usually amused or astonished when they're told that some game fish give off an odor — and striped bass smell like watermelon. Any fisherman who knows what he's doing will take advantage of this phenomenon. A good nose at sea is worth just as much as any fish-finding device ever created. And Cleveland had one of the best. She could smell a school of bass a mile upwind. This little red-haired girl from Shaker Heights had become a legend in her own time for her ability to sniff out schools of fish in a dense fog. When Cleveland said 'fish', you could bet on it.

Our sonar operator held his hand in the air as he bent over the machine. "Marking at 15 feet," he said, not taking his gaze away from the instrument. "Looks like bait."

Seawitch: *Anything underneath them?*

Captain Indian: *Yup, here they come now at 40 feet. Oh man! You guys look at this.*

We all huddled looking at the 40-foot line, while thin ones traced the paper from 10 to 15 feet.

Captain Magpie: *I think all hell's about to bust loose.*

Captain Indian: *Seawitch, swing over.*

I turned down the volume on the CB and reached for the VHF mic.

Seawitch: *Go ahead, Capt.*

Captain Indian: *You seeing the same thing we're seeing?*

Captain Magpie: *Yes, but we haven't had the first whack yet.*

Captain Indian: *You know that may be dogfish under those squid.*

Seawitch: *I doubt it. We just got a good indication that it isn't.*

Captain Indian: *How do you know for sure?*

Seawitch: *Cleveland just smelled watermelon.*

Captain Magpie: *That's a roger. Just sit tight; we smell the same thing.*

I was puzzled as to why the fish hadn't started to feed. Everything seemed perfect. All the factors appeared to be right, however, nothing was happening. It took a few minutes more before the missing part became apparent to me.

"I think it's slack water," announced Cleveland.

Seawitch: *That's it! You're right! They won't feed until the tide gets moving.*

9:30 a.m.

Four other charter boats from Barnstable, along with several private boats that follow us, began filtering into our fleet which now covered an area of almost two square miles. From the way some of the boats approached, I knew they were operated by people who lack the knowledge to find fish and were waiting on us to do it for them.

For these unexperienced skippers, locating fish on Cape Cod Bay boiled down to two choices. They could go off and try on their own or they could find and follow a charter boat and hope that the charter boat would lead them to fish. There's nothing wrong with this and most of the time, it proves beneficial to both parties, providing both give one another enough working room and a little courtesy.

I don't know of a charter boat skipper on the Cape who hasn't welcomed the call at one time or another from a private boat who has found feeding fish. However, there are always a few dense individuals in high-powered boats with low-powered brains that make everyone within their vicinity miserable. You could always spot these individuals by the way they approached a fleet of working boats that were over fish: they kept their throttles to the fire wall until they were in the center of the fleet and then they would set out lines and head for the stern of the nearest boat that was fighting fish. I knew that the sight of seven charter boats working the same area, along with other boats, would attract these ramrodders like a crowd to **Filene's Basement** on any given day.

9:40 a.m.

The radio traffic on the CB had reached a point when it was necessary to crank the volume up or squelch it completely. I had elected to do the second and was reaching for the set when Bob D., son of Jack Dillon, who was at the wheel, suddenly brought the Seawitch into a sharp starboard turn. Several seagulls swooped down from altitude and applied dive breaks over a reddish cloud of squid that was now racing toward our starboard beam a foot or so below the surface.

"Marking heavy at 20 feet," said John Mortimer. "We're right over big fish."

I quickly made a mental note of our position as the northern-most boat in relation to the fleet. I was about to tell Bob to pick up a little more speed when the port outrigger arched backward and snapped free.

"Go baby, go!" someone shouted.

Then, suddenly, a quarter square mile of bass erupted around us, tearing into the squid. It was as if the Seawitch had been set down in the center of a giant whirlpool. Bob D. threw us our gear, as every rod bent over and buckled to the tune of its grinding reel.

I waited a few seconds while everyone got their fish or fishes under control. It was a sure bet that some of the rods had doubled or even tripled. I grabbed a spinning rod out of the rack and headed for the pulpit. I made a medium-length cast and snapped the bail closed. The instant the plug hit the water I pumped the rod once and was rewarded with a powerful lunge that all but emptied the spool of 20-pound test line. There was nothing to do now but hang on and wait until my fish was ready to come in.

More than 40 boats to the south began swinging their bows toward us as the fish showed no sign of letting up on the squid. Two outboards several hundred yards to our stern had hooked up along with a sport fisherman to the west. They were almost rammed by a hot rodder that was hell bent on getting to me. The fact that he was running full speed over and through breaking fish hadn't occurred to him. The Seawitch was fighting fish, and by thunder that was where he was going.

Cleveland, without help, boated our first two 25-pound fish simply by gaffing one and lifting the other in by the head of the hoochie.

My fish spent his energy in a series of shallow half-moon runs and floated belly side beside Bob D., who stopped long enough from his own battle to gaff and drop him on the deck.

Within 10 minutes, six rods had accounted for 10 fish, almost 250 pounds of fish.

The hot rodder came galloping in and reined up almost 100 feet from our starboard side, just as we were ready to set out again.

Cleveland announced that she would run the boat and got us moving at a fast clip so that we could pay out lines quickly. The direction she chose was the same one hot rod used to get to us. Hundreds of fish were now erupting in his spent wake and Cleveland was going to take advantage of it.

"All out, Carrot top," said the John Mortimer.

Cleveland looked over her shoulder and simultaneously brought the Seawitch back to trolling speed.

"10, 9, 8, 7, 6 ..." she counted carefully, "5, 4, 3, tight."

Both outriggers wrapped back and popped free while the stern and port rods doubled over. Jack Dillon took the starboard wire and managed to get it within 30 feet of the stern when a bass in the 40-pound class stopped him dead in his tracks. This fish hit with such violence that the man lost his balance and went slamming into the back of a fighting chair that was being occupied by his son.

"Really, Dad?" Bob D. said, casually looking down at his father who had come to rest sitting in a pool of fish blood. "If you want this chair, all you have to do is ask."

10:15 am

From every point of the compass, fish could be seen rolling and breaking, sending white water flying as they plowed with gaping mouths through schools of stricken squid. Boats had given up trying to hone in on one another because there was no need to.

At one point while we were stopped, I took a look through the binoculars at a vast area of breaking fish to the southeast that not a single boat had gotten to. All but a few of the hot rods had given up racing around and started catching fish. How long this action would last was anybody's guess, but one thing was certain: the word was out.

On Cape Cod, the most popular daytime entertainment is not television soap operas, it's citizen band radio. Don't think for a minute that Cape Coders spend a lot of time talking to one another on the sets or even care to. Many thousand set owners hardly ever key the mic, but our dear friends who do listen, day after day, season after season, listen to what they call the best program on the air: the charter boat fleet. If Captain Magpie got locked out of his house for a night, or Captain Tramp's son cut his first tooth, or Cleveland showed up in the morning in open-toed wedges with a parasol, it's known from Race Point to Plymouth. Thousands of people over several hundred square miles spend their days laughing and working with us, the captains and the crew, and can usually tell you what happened to who or what was caught where.

A few years ago, a very famous TV writer and his wife stopped me while I was shopping in the Barnstable news store one afternoon and introduced themselves. I asked them how they knew me?

"Well, we saw your t-shirt and assumed you were the captain, and we listen on the radio."

"Oh," I said laughing. "That explains it."

"Well, we think it's wonderful. It's grand entertainment," they said thoughtfully.

"Well I'm glad you're pleased," I said. "But I'm sure what you do is better."

"No, I refuse to believe that," the man said. "What I do is all make believe, but when I'm listening to the boats, I'm listening to the real thing. Action, mystery, adventure, drama, and danger. It's live and we feel that we're part of it."

I couldn't disagree with the man because lots of others have said the same. However, being part of it meant a lot more to several hundred private boat owners and their crews than just tuning in the CB. The words, "they're up," "they're blitzing," or "breaking fish" on the CB instantly galvanized this armada into action. And soon, hundreds of boats of every size, shape, and description would head our way.

From the way things were now shaping up, I doubted anyone who came out here would go back empty-handed, as fish were feeding with unparalleled intensity over 11 square miles.

11:30 a.m.

Four passes with our conventional trolling gear had netted us 20 fish from 15 to 45 pounds. Everyone, including myself, decided that we've had enough of that; it was now time to bring a little dignity to what was otherwise becoming a vulgar brawl.

Spinning rods with single hook plugs would do nicely and before long, we settled into a nice routine of drifting and casting into breaking fish. We worked with four rods in a clockwise manner. Two people forward of the pulpit and bow would cast. As soon as they hooked up, they worked their fish aft and other anglers would take their place.

After a while, Cleveland and I regulated ourselves to de-hooking and gaffing duties, as I was sure we had taken near the amount that this crew would need.

"How many fish will it take to do the job?" I shouted to John Mortimer as he stepped to the end of the pulpit.

"30 or so will be just fine," he said, sending his plug flying. "I don't think we want many more than that."

"Well you better not get another one," Cleveland said lifting a bucket of water over the side. "Cause we got over 40."

"Don't worry about it," Jack Dillon said. "When those nuns see this load, they'll promote us to pope or something."

"Good heavens! I wasn't keeping track," John Mortimer said, coming back on deck. "Let's get out of here and get this stuff cleaned and iced down."

Boats of every description from every harbor and launching ramp on Cape Cod Bay could be seen working fish as we slow-trolled our way in. From a distance, it looked like a shiny new city had risen out of the sea and stood drying and waxing in the noon-time sun. Rods and equipment were stowed below as the Seawitch changed from a fishing machine into a processing plant. An assembly line was set up and fish were quickly scaled, gutted, washed, and packed away.

Captain Lobster: *Did you get **saved**?*

He asked as we pulled into his wake in the channel.

Seawitch: ***Finest kind****. Thanks for the mild indication.*

Captain Indian: *Yeah. Well I didn't see bass, but when I saw those squid I knew the crap would hit the fan.*

It was a little after 1 p.m. when we tied up. 48 stripers were aboard representing almost 1,200 pounds of fresh protein that a lot of grateful people would enjoy.

The blitz ended shortly after our return.

Captain Magpie: *It was like somebody turned off the switch. Today was almost perfect.*

Seawitch: *What do you mean, almost? It was perfect.*

Captain Magpie: *Like hell! I didn't get to see Cleveland in that new green bikini.*

Chapter 6

~~~~~~

Storm

It happened that a bad squall blew up.
The waves were breaking over the boat,
And it began to ship water badly.

(Saint Joseph Edition of the New American Bible, Mark 4: 37)

In "The Divine Comedy," Dante depicts a hell that is segmented and compartmentalized, where divine retribution is precisely tailored to fit the offender's crime. So, if this be the case and it very well may be, I'm sure our Maker, in his infinite wisdom, has set aside one whole division where false prophets, soothsayers, astrologers, crystal ballers, and other of the same like are going to get their comeuppance. Now, I'm hoping that in the very lowest and very hottest place in this division, there is a special department reserved for the worst offenders of them all: the local TV and radio weather forecasters. No punishment is too bad for these fiends. No pitch fork too sharp and no demons too nasty for this bunch of Cassandras. One fitting punishment I can think of is that they are made to stand naked in public in the weather they predict incorrectly, or perhaps they should be tied to their satellites.

The following examples may be used by those of you unaccustomed to the Cape's weather, so that in some small way you may learn to expect the unexpected when visiting our fair shores.

A day in early April; the forecast: partly cloudy with rising temperatures up to the low 40s. In the afternoon, a 10 percent chance of a spring shower in coast lying areas. Have a nice day folks.

Yes, folks. We had a nice day. We spent the day shoveling six inches of partly cloudy off the deck in 25-degree weather.

A Friday in mid-July; the forecast: variable breezes from the southeast with 8- to 10-mile per hour winds. Some chance of showers in the morning. Looks like another great weekend for all you beach bunnies out there. Don't forget to take it easy if you're just starting your tan.

We didn't see the sun for three days. That gentle southeast wind went north-east with gusts up to 50 knots, with torrential down pours from Montaug to Maine. All those beach bunnies spent their weekend warranted up in a monumental traffic jam around the local shopping malls praying that their skin wouldn't mildew before they left Cape Cod.

On a Friday, in mid-June, the forecast was rain beginning late this after-noon and lasting well into Sunday; temperatures in the 60s with southwest wind, 15 to 25 knots. Sorry folks, but maybe we'll have better news for you later in the week.

The words from "The Rime of the Ancient Mariner" just about sums this one up:

> Day by day, day by day,
>   We stuck, nor breath nor motion;
> As idle as a painted ship
>   Upon a painted ocean

Motels and restaurants went begging. Beaches were almost deserted, and charter boats sat idle in the hot sun. Everyone lost on this one.

A person would think that with all the modern technology, computer, and orbiting satellites and heaven knows what else that these weather people would be accurate at least 95 percent of the time. The stone-cold truth is that in the last 20 years their accuracy and credibility has slipped to a point on our charts that one would describe as slightly lower than whale manure.

There is not a week during the season that I'm not on the phone convincing new customers to disregard the local television and radio weathermen, and to come down or stay home, whatever the case.

The lost income to charter captains and missed fishing days to sportsmen because of inaccurate weather forecasting is disheartening. However, if this were the only case and all that was lost was time and money then it wouldn't be so bad, but now and again, lives are lost.

The following narrative isn't pleasant. What is so sad is that it's a story that gets repeated time and time again each year.

––––––

It began on a late May morning in the early 1970s. I was in the process of loading customers and gear aboard for a day of ground fishing when my mate handed me the CB mic.

"It's Capt. Lobster. Wants to know if we're on the way yet," she said.

Seawitch: *About five minutes. How's it look?*

Captain Lobster: *You get the marine weather yet?*

Seawitch: *Yes, but I haven't got a fresh update, so I'm going to watch it.*

Captain Lobster: *You want to hear what the TV guy said this morning?*

Seawitch: *Okay, I'll bite.*

Captain Lobster: *Well the son of a bitch said we're going to get 5 to 10 westerly swinging south this afternoon; going to be gentle and variable.*

Seawitch: *What do you say?*

Captain Lobster: *Hang on to your ass. I'm not going any farther than my third string of pots. How far you going?*

Seawitch: *I'm flounder fishing, and I'll be anchored up in back of the neck.*

Captain Lobster: *Get the marine weather and call me back. I got to grab one.*

Cleveland had been listening to the marine station with her ear to the speaker. "15 to 25 northwest, with gusts up to 40," she said in a flat voice, wrinkling up her nose.

I keyed the CB mic and repeated the forecast to Captain Lobster.

Captain Lobster: *My God! Those silly bastards on TV must be in some other world. I wish to hell they would get it straight for once!*

My customers had been listening to our conversation and wanted to know if the conditions would be OK for their trip.

I explained that we would be less than a mile from our dock and that we'd anchored in a small cove in the inner harbor, less than 50 yards from the back beach out of the wind.

"Great!" they said, looking somewhat more than relieved. "Have we got time to grab some breakfast? We didn't stop on the way down."

"Sure," I said, "we got plenty of time, go ahead."

Cleveland had been giving me her starving, wounded puppy look.

"Take my mate with you," I said. "She hasn't been fed this week."

Everyone burst into laughter, including Cleveland who managed to slip me a half of a V-for-victory salute as she and the crew made their way up the gang way.

I went back to the CB and told Captain Lobster what the situation was, and I would be out shortly.

> Captain Lobster: *It's going to come. I figure when the tide starts out we're going to get it, and open water is no place to be.*

I agreed with him and spent a few more minutes talking to a charter boat captain in **Plymouth** who explained that this crew would be fishing close to his harbor whether they liked it or not.

Angel Base came on the air and instructed us that she had been talking to several boats off **Provincetown**, and they were making a run for shore.

A Rock Harbor skipper came back with the statement that his fleet was going to spend their day inside **Wellfleet,** and he didn't know of anyone, charter or private, who was going to be outside.

I busied myself cutting clams and sea worms into hook size portions, all the while regretting that I didn't ask Cleveland to bring me back a coffee and donut.

"Sir," a voice floated down at me from the bulkhead.

I looked up into the face of a pretty young lady wearing a yellow windbreaker.

"Can I help you?" I asked, smiling back.

"My father and mother would like to know where the Barnstable launching ramp is," she said, pushing her long dark hair out of her face.

I started to point but thought better of it. "I'll be right up," I said, washing my hands in a bucket of sea water.

I met the pretty teen at the top of the gangway and walked her over to a running station wagon with a 20-foot outboard in tow.

"My name's Susan, we're from Albany, and my dad's a doctor; are you a real sea captain?" she asked all in one breath.

"I guess," I said. "Do I look like one?"

"You sure do. Love your beard," she added.

"Are you on vacation?" I asked.

"Yes, it's great! I go to a private school and the pipes broke and they let us out early."

"I never was that lucky when I was a kid," I said. "I used to pray that the school would burn down."

"Susan's a chatter box," her mother said, getting out of the station wagon. "You'll have to forgive her."

"Well, she's a pretty chatter box," I said offering my hand to her father who was sliding out from behind the driver's seat. "Are you going fishing?" I asked. "Or just out for a boat ride?"

"They're going fishing," said Susan's mom, pointing to her husband and another man who had gotten out of the back seat.

"What kind of fishing?" I asked, looking over their boat.

"We're interested in striped bass. When we were on the Cape last year, the man at the tackle shop said Barnstable was a good place to start looking."

"It is," I said. "But I don't recommend you go out today unless you stay inside and bottom fish. We're expecting some high winds, and you could get in trouble."

"We watched the weather forecast last night," said Susan's dad, the doctor. "And again, this morning. Both said it's going to be nice for the next two days."

"What kinds of station did you watch?" I questioned.

"The television," he said, appearing a little annoyed.

"And we just got it on the car radio," added the other man, Susan's uncle, with a bright skeptical smile. "What makes you disagree?"

"First of all," I said. "The VHF marine weather is giving a different forecast that doesn't look good, and from years of experience we have learned not to rely on standard radio or television forecasts. They're just not that accurate."

"What makes the VHF any different from the television?" her dad questioned, looking more skeptical than ever.

"Professional meteorologists and the United States Coast Guard," I said. "The weather reports given out are about as accurate as you can get, and even then, we have to watch it."

"Well, it's a beautiful morning, the sun's out, and there's no wind to speak of," he continued. "I think we'll be OK."

"Would you like to listen on my boat's radio?" I offered.

"No thanks. I'm sure we'll be OK. We spend a lot of time up on the Finger Lakes. We know what to look for," added the uncle.

"This isn't a lake," I said. "It's a bay, part of the North Atlantic. You can get into real trouble if you're not careful."

"Well, I'm sure we all appreciate your concern," said her dad, with a condescending note in his voice. "We'll be careful. Our boat can do 40 miles per hour, and it won't take us long to get back if the weather goes bad."

I looked at the tri-hull construction of their boat and it's two 100-horse power outboards. "Not in a six-foot sea," I said flatly. This didn't bring a response from either man.

"Would you show us the launching ramp?" asked Susan's father, forcing a smile.

I pointed across the harbor. "Right between the two buildings."

He managed a 'thank you', still holding his forced smile.

"You got a radio?" I asked.

"Sure, we got a portable," he answered.

I hadn't noticed an antenna mount on their boat and I was curious. "You might think about putting one on," I said. "They come in handy.

"All you get is truck drivers asking for the time of day," stated Susan's uncle.

"I'll agree with that," I said. "But you might want to think about a marine radio if you're going to spend any time on the ocean."

"It wouldn't be worth it," Susan's dad answered. "We only go on salt water a few times a year."

At this point I figured I'd said enough: I'm sure from their point of view I was probably just an irritating know-it-all trying to impress them as some sort of authority on something that they weren't all that concerned about. After all, it was a bright, clear morning with no wind to speak of, and those high broom tailed clouds didn't mean a thing.

"Be careful and good luck," I said, turning and walking back toward the Seawitch.

Susan waved and smiled. "Goodbye, Captain," she said as she and her family got into their station wagon.

I was to see her once more in years to come, but that smile would never ever again be the same.

Angel Base was on the air with Captain Lobster when I got back aboard.

Angel Base: *I talked to a dragger somewhere near the Maryann buoy. And he's got 10 to 15 northwest.*

Plymouth charter boat: *It's just a matter of time. It's going to come fellas, it's going to come.*

Cleveland and company came thundering down the gangway, and in 25 minutes we were anchored up safely behind Sandy neck catching yellowtails.

Seawitch: *Have you seen a tri-hull outboard?*

Angel Base: *Seawitch, he'll be back in a minute. He's taking bait or talking to his bait man on another channel.*

After a few minutes, the radio came to life.

Captain Lobster: *I'm here, Bob. I see him. He's trolling down inside the channel. He's in a good spot there.*

Seawitch: *Thank heavens! I warned them about the weather on the dock. I'm glad they listened.*

Captain Lobster: *Well, if he stays inside where he's at now, he'll be fine.*

Angel Base: *Does he have a radio, Seawitch?*

Seawitch: *No.*

Angel Base: *Well I hope he's smart enough to stay inside.*

Seawitch: *I hope so too.*

The next half hour or so was uneventful, except for an incident when an excited customer reeled a flounder all the way up to the tip of his rod and stood holding the flopping fish out over the water.

"Are you going to bring it in?" Cleveland asked in a pleasant voice. "Or climb out on your rod and stab it to death?"

Plymouth charter boat: *Hold on to your hats, cousins! We just got hit with a gust about 40 knots.*

Captain Lobster: *You got that, Angel?*

Angel Base: *I got it. You on, Seawitch?*

Seawitch: *I'm on, Angel.*

Captain Lobster: *Bob, look to the northwest.*

I hadn't been paying attention to the horizon, but I now gave it my full attention. The complete northwest quadrant of the sky was turning a greenish dark gray with tumbling, dirty-white cotton ball clouds streaking out ahead of us.

Seawitch: *I hope you're on your way, Captain.*

Captain Lobster: *I got this damn slab firewalled.*

Seawitch: *How far down are you?*

Captain Lobster: *I just passed No. 3 buoy. I'll see you in 10 minutes.*

Seawitch: *Is that outboard anywhere near you?*

There was a few moments pause before the radio came back to life.

Captain Lobster: *No, I don't see him. He was down by No. 6 a little while ago. I hope to God's sake he's inside.*

My crew had stopped fishing momentarily and began stuffing themselves into rain gear.

"Has anyone seen an outboard go by?" I asked, getting everyone's attention.

Everyone looked at everyone else and no one answered.

"What outboard?" questioned Cleveland.

Captain Lobster: *Hold on, Seawitch! It just hit us!*

I quickly looked out from under our canvas top and noticed that a few puff balls had passed us. I was thinking what strange phenomenon it was to see scud go flying by so close and not feel the wind, when a gust hit us with such force that sand from the beach flew up in our eyes. It was about 50 yards away and slammed into us with BB shot-like velocity. That first blast of air had to have been in excess of 50 knots, and that was after it had jumped itself over a damn good size peninsula that stood between us and open water.

I started the Seawitchs' diesel and let it idle in case our anchor pulled free of its line part. However, the oversize Danfork anchor with its 10 feet of chain and one-inch polypropylene did its job and kept us safely in our small cove.

The sky went black with rain that instantly replaced the sand storm. The best way to describe its effects is to imagine one's self and crew as the losing side in a tug of war at a fireman's picnic.

Angel put out a call to Captain Lobster to see if he was OK, and it was a full 30 seconds before the radio crackled back.

Captain Lobster: *Stand by, Angel.*

I knew that from the way he answered that he was taking a beating coming down the channel.

Visibility had dropped to something less than 100 yards in the rain, wind, and spray, making any navigation at all a nightmare. I had been too busy to think about the outboard, but when I did, fear, dread, and a sense of uselessness filled me. In time it would leave me, but the uneasy sense of guilt that would replace it would take a lot longer to depart. The chances of a 20-foot outboard surviving that wind-torn sea was next to impossible. The wake of events that were leftover from this day would take life times to erase, and that pretty little face with her dark hair and friendly smile would haunt me for years. Perhaps I should have tried harder to explain to them about our weather. If I had only done this. If I ... If ...

Someone once said never get in the way of a man who's determined and hell-bent on his own destruction. Well, I got in the way of these two men, and I'll never be sorry I did; I only wish I had succeeded in stopping them.

Captain Lobster rounded the point at full throttle, kicking spray high in the air. He killed the power the second he made the cove and came sliding up to us.

I keyed the mic and told Angel he was OK.

Angel Base: *Did you see that outboard?*

Seawitch: *No, Angel, I didn't. He may have seen the weather coming and got back by us without us seeing him.*

Captain Lobster: *He wasn't in the channel. I looked real good and he either went in or out, and I hope for his sake he went in.*

Several calls for assistance, along with two maydays came over the VHF. Many anxious calls arrived on the CB from shore-based stations seeking reassurance that this boat or that boat was inside and safe. The Coast Guard and Angel Base had their hands full.

One woman in a yacht anchored up in Provincetown harbor was screaming frantically to the Coast Guard that her dog had been washed overboard, and her brother-in-law was in Congress, so they had damn well better find her dog. The young Coast Guardsman kept his cool through her tirade, reassuring her that everything possible would be done to help her locate her dog, but people came first, and there were people in trouble; for now she would just have to wait. The woman seemed to calm herself somewhat and gave the Coast Guard a detailed description of a miniature poodle with a rhinestone collar that answered to the name of Wiggles. The thought of powerful cutters crashing through storm-tossed seas calling for Wiggles was just about all I could take.

The rain slacked off a bit, but the wind remained at gale force, never dropping below 30 knots and occasionally gusting up to 45.

Captain Lobster, who owns a **mooring** in the cove, tied up to it and spent the next two hours sorting out the mess of tangled gear and overturned equipment that his ride in from open water produced.

My crew, obviously undaunted by the weather, were filling their bags with the yellowtails that were feeding intently through the storm.

Angel and I contacted the owner of the outboard marina in our harbor and told him our fears. We gave him a description of the outboard and the station wagon and trailer, as we wanted to make sure, one way or another, before we alerted the Coast Guard.

Marina operator: *I know who you're talking about. Those people asked to leave their trailer here for the day. I'll send one of the boys to see if it's still here.*

While we waited for his call, I had time to tell Cleveland the story, and her face went bleach white; she knew that no small boat would have much of a chance in that sea.

In a short while, the marina operator was back on the air.

Marina operator: *Their trailer's gone. They must have come in.*

I breathed a sigh of relief, and I'm sure Captain Lobster and Angle Base did the same. However, this was short-lived, for in a few days I would know the truth.

The wind dropped off a little at low tide that afternoon, and we made our short run back to the harbor.

There would be no fishing for the next two days, as Cleveland was graduating from college, and I had work at home to take care of. Several people along the New England seaboard had been killed during that storm, and the Coast Guard was busy for days after looking for the missing. It wasn't until the afternoon of the following Monday that I learned the true fate of the two men from Albany. A young Coast Guardsman in a pickup truck was sent to Barnstable to look for an overdue 40-foot sail boat. I found the boat for him tied up inside the Basin.

"Thanks Captain," he said. "Always someone forgetting to tell where they are."

I nodded in agreement.

"By the way, we're looking for a twin outboard with two men from up-state New York. It was reported missing out of Wellfleet harbor a few days ago right after the storm.

"A doctor from Albany and one other guy?" I said, beginning to feel sick.

"Yes," he said.

"That boat didn't go out of Wellfleet. It went out of here," I said.

By that evening I had the full story. The trailer was never left in **Barnstable**. The doctor's wife told the Coast Guard that the men changed their minds and decided to fish in Barnstable, then run across the bay to Wellfleet and pull there, as it was nearer to their cottage. She said they had charts and knew how to use a compass. And they told her that it wouldn't take much more than a half hour to get to Wellfleet with their speed and after all why should she bother driving all the way back to Barnstable to pick them up. When they didn't return when they said they would, she didn't worry because she could see several boats fishing inside Wellfleet harbor. She assumed they were just a little late but were OK. It wasn't until late afternoon that she went to the harbormaster at Wellfleet and reported her husband and brother missing. The Coast Guard searched for several days, but not a trace of the boat or a body was ever recovered.

That summer slipped by and on top of it the years. I never forgot that day, but I learned to place it in its proper perspective of things and live with it. However, the thought of Susan, that dark-haired girl, and what she had to live through never settled with me.

It was on an early September afternoon, a decade later, that a tall young woman came up to me as I was about to go down to the boat.

"Are you the captain of the Seawitch?" she asked with a shy note in her voice.

"Yes ma'am," I said, smiling back.

"You don't remember me," she said. "But I met you once a long time ago."

"You're very kind," I said. "I've been doing this a long time, and I've met thousands of people."

"It was the day my father died," she said looking intently at me. "I was just 13, a little girl."

I gazed back at her face for a moment and then remembered.

"You're Susan, and you're from Albany, New York," I said impulsively reaching out and touching her long dark hair.

We talked for the better part of an hour. Her mother had eventually re-married after many terrible years of nervous breakdowns and psychological readjustments. There had been a somewhat awful battle to recoup her father's insurance as the company wasn't sure he was dead. They had to wait a long time, she explained. All the Coast Guard would say was that he was missing and presumed dead. They ended up selling their home and mov-ing into a modest apartment, as there was never enough money. Leaving her neighborhood and friends and starting public school was difficult, but Susan did fine. I didn't like the public school at first, she said, but after a while I loved it because it was more fun. Her uncle's family went through pretty much the same thing, only her aunt had to go to work right away to support their three children and hadn't remarried.

"Why did you come back?" I asked.

Susan pushed her hair from her face momentarily marshalling her thoughts. "I wanted to see where it happened," she said. "I remembered the name of your boat and somehow, someday I knew that I had to come back."

"I understand," I said.

"Would you take me out there?" Susan asked. "I'll pay you."

Pay me, I thought. My God! Hasn't she paid enough?

"Sure, we'll take a run out, and I won't accept payment."

The late afternoon sun glinted gold in our wake as blue-green waters flooded over the bars into the channel. I cut power at about the halfway point and killed the engine, letting the tide drift us seaward. Turns and gulls cried and played tag in the flame blue sky as we slipped quietly into their world of air and water.

Susan looked about her, then fixed her gaze on the vast empty horizon. Tears were on her cheeks and she started to brush them aside.

"Leave them alone," I said opening my arms to her. I held her tight a long moment listening to the deep, soft sobs that came from the very core of her soul.

"I guess it's time I said goodbye to him and my uncle. I could never give them up before," she whispered.

I smiled and looked down into that tearful, pretty face. She knew that I understood.

Her gaze went back to the horizon for a moment, back to that endless plain. "When I was a child, I always wondered why the sea is so big," Susan said.

I thought for a moment, then caught her gaze. "Why, that's because it's where all the tears have gathered since the beginning of time," I answered.

Chapter 7

Is That a Haddock?

Cold sleet was beating an icy tattoo on the hood of my pickup as it crunched alongside the dock at 6:30 a.m. I switched off the engine when something wearing a set of orange and yellow oil skins over two turtleneck sweaters, two pairs of pants, and a goose down jacket with boots and gloves came waddling up to the driver's side and made a motion to me to roll down the window.

"Good morning," I said cheerfully. "What a lovely May morning."

The thing held up a gloved hand with three fingers extended.

"Is that some form of greeting or salute?" I asked.

Cleveland shook the sleet off a carrot she was eating and glared at me. I could tell it was her because a lock of red hair had escaped from under her wool cap and played tag with the tip of her turned up nose.

"Yes, it's a salute and it's also a greeting. Want to know what it means?" Cleveland teased.

I nodded the affirmative.

"It means peace but screw you anyway," she said in a firm voice.

"Oh!" I exclaimed, trying to hold back my laughter and look bewildered.

"Want a bite?" she asked.

"No thanks," I answered.

"Get the weather yet?" she wondered.

"Yes," I said. "Those stupid bastards have done it again."

"100 percent wrong. Right?" she laughed.

"Yeah, this makes it four days straight they're wrong," I replied.

You would think with all the modern devices and satellites that they would at least give an educated guess.

Cleveland shrugged her shoulders and bit hard into her carrot. "Our people were there early," she said. "They went to get coffees."

"Good. You got everything set?" I asked.

Cleveland managed to munch out a 'yes'.

"OK, but there's something I just have to tell you before we push off. Hope you don't mind," I explained.

Munch, munch.

"You're a pretty kid, but your mother dresses you funny," I joked.

At that moment I couldn't tell what Cleveland's expression was, for somehow a half-eaten carrot was shoved into my mouth.

Little gray puffs of spin drifts floated over us as we nudged away from the dock and slipped quietly past lines of tied up vessels. I turned up the volume on our VHF and switched on our second radio, a 120-channel single side ban CB, and set the depth alarm for six feet.

Seawitch: *Good morning, Angel Base.*

A few seconds passed, then a familiar friendly voice answered.

Angel Base: *You on the way, Captain?*

Seawitch: *Yes ma'am, but it looks like we'll need ice skates.*

Angel Base: *Well, at least you don't have wind.*

Plymouth lobster boat: *Thank God for small favors.*

Angel Base: *Okay fellows, I'm going to finish my coffee. I'll be standing by if you need me.*

I looked out over the bow and watched the sleet hiss into the sea. "What's the water temperature?" I shouted back to Cleveland.

My mate said something to a tall, gray man in a faded rain jacket, and he worked his way forward.

"I figure we'd have about 15 minutes if we went in," he said.

"What is it?" I asked.

"47 degrees. Too cold for a swim," Cleveland explained.

Mr. White was right. 15 minutes would be about it. I quietly thanked God for Angel Base. For many years this wonderful woman had saved both hundreds of people's lives and their property by staying close to her radio. Her home was located high on a cliff overlooking 400 square miles of Cape Cod Bay, and from this vantage point she was able to monitor radio traffic and weather for all the fishing fleet and private traffic. She never accepted a penny for her time and had often said that being able to save lives and help people was all the pay she would ever need. She had become a vital link between us and the Coast Guard, and they loved her for the part she played. The minute a mayday or call for assistance came over the CB, Angel would get a description and location of the vessel, then direct the nearest available boat to the rescue. This not only saved time, it also lessened the load on the Coast Guard and saved the taxpayers thousands of dollars each year.

I can readily recall some 20 different incidents in the past 10 years where the Seawitch and Angel Base teamed up for a rescue. Had that friendly voice not sought us out, several people would not be here today.

"You know something, Captain? I'll never get used to seeing these trees," gray-haired, Mr. White said, leaning forward and looking at the twin line of pine trees that jutted out of the water that marked the basin entrance in the harbor.

"Of all the damn things to use. If I didn't know better, I would swear that they grew there," he continued.

The old man laughed a little as he had heard my usual reply to several of his friends over the years, which was that these trees were rare Pinus Oceananis, the only pine tree in the world that grows in salt water. A whole shipping industry was involved to barge in tons of whale manure to keep them fertilized. This explanation was always good for a few laughs, as most folks quickly realized that the only manure these trees got was the brand the captain was spreading. Actually, with our normal 11-foot tides and swift cross-counter currents, the tall, thin pines were the only things that would last. Buoys, barrels, and cut lumber were tried, along with a host of other things, but the 20-foot willowy pines that were harvested in a nearby forest and driven in each spring proved to be the best.

"We may have a little trouble," Mr. White said quietly.

"We brought a new man. I'm sure he's been drinking a little, and I don't believe he's ever fished. I didn't want to bring him, but he's a relative of my business partner, and I couldn't refuse.

"That's OK," I said. "I'm sure he'll be fine. We'll take good care of him."

The old man thanked me with a nod of his head.

"Want to take the wheel a spell?" I asked, slipping from behind the station.

Mr. White said, "Sure," stepping behind the wheel to take over.

I watched him check the compass, scan the instrument panel, then bring the Seawitch into a sweeping wide starboard turn, past the harbor entrance light, pointing her bow down the channel.

I went off to greet our newest angler, who at the moment appeared to be trying to swallow a 16-ounce beer can.

"How many has he had?" I asked Cleveland, who was busy quartering sea worms on the bait tank lid.

"I'm not sure," she said harpooning another worm, "but I know he hasn't stopped since we got under way.

Mr. White's son was standing nearby and held up seven fingers, rolling his eyes skyward.

I nodded to him that I would take care of the situation and made my way over to where the new man, Joseph Murphy, was digging into an ice-filled chest for his eighth beer.

"Good morning," I said offering my hand as he straightens up with his prize.

"Oh, hi. Which one of you guys is the captain?" Joseph said, blinking and belching at the same time.

I realized that with the mountain of clothing Cleveland was wearing, even a sober person would have trouble believing that inside that get-up was a slim, attractive young woman.

"He is," I whispered into the man's ear and pointed back at Cleveland. "I hope you can handle your booze because the captain don't take kindly to guys who can't hold their liquor. He doesn't mind if you drink, but you better not cause trouble."

"Oh, I wouldn't do that. I can hold it. Believe me," said Joseph.

I went on to tell him that the captain wanted him to have an enjoyable day and catch a lot of fish for his family, so he should be careful not to get sick or hurt himself.

He smiled and took another swig of beer. "Look, I'm gonna be just fine, but I want to make sure I catch some haddock. We gonna catch a lot of haddock, ain't we?"

"I doubt it," I told him. "We're not going for haddock. They're out in deep water, and we'll be fishing in close for flounder, cod, and pollock. Very seldom do you get haddock where we are going."

"Well, the hell with that other shit. I want a haddock!" Joseph demanded.

"Well friend, you're going to have to trust in luck to try and catch one because the man who booked and paid for this trip wants flounder and cod."

"Damn," he mumbled taking his beer in both hands sitting down. "I want a haddock."

I started to make my way aft to see how Cleveland was coming along with the bait when I found him standing up, reaching out to pull me back.

"What's wrong?" I asked.

"Him! What the hell is he doing?" Joseph said pointing his beer at the man behind the wheel.

"Running the boat," I answered.

"Well I hope to hell he knows what he's doing. I got a wife and kids!" he exclaimed.

"Don't worry," I answered him back. "I think he told the captain that he once took a lesson at a summer camp or was a Sea Scout or something."

"Oh my God! You guys are nuts! We'll be killed! Take me back! I want to go back!" Joseph demanded.

"OK, but first we have to get a load of fish. Then I'll ask the captain to bring us back in. How's that sound?" Cleveland explained.

"OK, I guess" he said, turning his head toward the other members of the party.

Those in hearing distance nodded assurance and Joseph seemed to relax a little.

"I hope I get a haddock," he said, as I turned again to go forward, but when I looked back he was fishing in the cooler for another beer.

"How's my guest?" Mr. White asked when I came forward.

"He's a little worried about your experience, so I told him you were a Sea Scout."

The old man smiled then laughed out loud. "You know, I actually was. My last two years in high school and before I left for Annapolis, I worked setting up a Sea Scout program."

"Was it at a summer camp?" I asked with a grin.

"Sure was, Captain. We were on a big lake." Mr. White added.

I thought a moment, then put my hand on the old man's shoulder. "You know, Admiral, I wonder if God charges it up as a sin when you tell a lie that turns out to be the truth."

Mr. White laughed again and said that he felt we would still get docked for it because at the time, we knew it was a lie. However, he thought that a good defense attorney might give it a run for its money.

At that moment, the radio interrupted.

Angel Base: *Seawitch, are you ready for a weather up-date?*

Seawitch: *Go ahead, sweetheart. Let's hear what the soothsayers have got this time.*

Angel Base: *Well, they're saying that we are now enjoying 65 degrees Fahrenheit, and we have a sunny day ahead of us with a cold front coming in tomorrow.*

Seawitch: *Angel?*

Angel Base: *Yeah, Seawitch?*

Seawitch: *Would you like to make an obscene phone call for us to the weather bureau?*

Angel Base: *Sure thing, Captain.*

Seawitch: *OK, you can tell them that we have their partly sunny on our deck, and it's cold and slippery as hell.*

Angel Base: *OK.*

Then a dragger working out of Wellfleet came on the air, along with the lobster boat off Plymouth. They both asked Angel in so many words to convey their own special greeting to the weather people.

The old man stepped from behind the wheel. "I'm going back and see how Joseph is. Besides I wouldn't want to get us lost."

Some Sea Scout, I thought as I traded places. I know that a lot of the guests the old man invited aboard had little or no idea of his background, other than he was the chairman of the board of a large corporation and that once, he had been in the Navy. However, all one had to do was read a little history and they would soon find that this pleasant gentleman had been more than instrumental placing half the Japanese Imperial fleet on the bottom of the Pacific.

Cleveland came forward and nodded an all set. Bait was cut and six light rods were rigged with two-hook flounders spreaders with 8-ounce leads.

I brought the Seawitch into a tight turn to port working back against the tide and slowed the engine as we came alongside a marker buoy that put us in four fathoms of water, over a stone and sand bottom.

Cleveland dropped the anchor and in less than five minutes; four of the six rods were busy with yellowtails.

"Should I go back and work with him?" Cleveland asked while we watched with interest as the Joseph tried to decide which was more important: the cigarette he was trying to light; the 16-ounce beer can that, somehow, he couldn't let go of; or the arched-over rod that was bouncing under his arm.

"No," I said laughing. "I'll work with him. Besides he thinks you're a guy, and I told him you were the captain."

"No damn wonder he keeps giving me these funny looks." Mr. White answered.

I quickly made my way back to where the crisis had reached a standstill while Cleveland went below in search of a carrot and a cup of hot chocolate.

"Well old friend, sometimes it's hard to choose just what pleasure we want to indulge in first," I said, taking the rod from under Joseph's arm.

"Hey! I think I got a fish on."

"I'm sure you have. Why don't you set your beer down, light your cigarette, and you can bring him in?"

"I don't know how. I've never fished before."

"Okay, just watch what I do for a couple of seconds, then you can take over."

I gave the rod a few pumps, then handed it back to him. Surprisingly he did well, and in a few seconds, a lovely eight-pound silver and olive pollock was gaffed and lifted aboard.

"Is that a haddock?" Joseph questioned, obviously delighted with the fish.

Something clicked in my brain. "Why do you want a haddock?" I asked with the biggest disarming smile I could muster.

"Ain't for me. We don't like fish. It's for the old lady next door. She has cats, and she said they like haddock, so when I told her I was going out on a boat, she made me promise that I would bring her back a haddock. I couldn't give a shit, but she babysits for nothing."

"Well, congratulations," I said slapping him on the shoulder. "You won't disappoint her. I'll personally clean and skin the haddock for you so that her little kittens won't get bones."

At this point, I thought a few of the crew might let the cat out of the bag, but everyone seemed very relieved that he had caught his "haddock."

The rest of the trip was a simple exercise in market fishing. After five hours, we had close to 400 pounds of flounder, cod, blackfish, and several 'pollock-haddock.' A few minutes after docking, the sun came out, turning a dripping gray atmosphere into a beautiful, warm spring afternoon. Cleveland stood by the ramp and said a few words to each man as they made their way up to the parking lot. She had taken off her jacket and wool hat, letting a mop of red hair spill over her shoulders.

"Thanks for coming," she said, smiling as Joseph came abreast of her.

He shook his head for a moment and broke into a broad grin. "Boy, lady," he said. "You should have been out there with us. I got this big haddock."

Chapter 8

The Reunion

The first time I saw Homer Adams Lewis was on a late November day over a decade and a half ago. As I remember it, I was hunting a snow-covered ridge in Woodstock, Vermont, and he was sitting with his back against one of the few hemlocks that dotted an otherwise hill of Beech and Maple trees. I was about 50 yards from his location.

"Did you shoot while back?" I asked, noticing that his rifle had its lever jacked open.

"That I did," he answered, pointing to a five-point buck that lay a few yards down from the hill from him. "Come on over and sit a spell. I got some coffee left."

I walked down the hill and saw that he had dressed and tagged the deer. "Congratulations," I said. "You waiting for help to drag him out?"

"No, it just arrived," he laughed. "You're a strong looking boy. You'll do just fine."

"Sure, why not," I said, taking the thermos he offered.

"Good," he said. "We can sit, and swap lies. Besides, I'm not in a hurry. I kinda like watching the snow fall, don't you?"

The friendship that began that late November day almost 17 years ago lasted until his death, which was within a few months of this writing. I shall miss him, but in a sense, Homer will never be far away, for his rich legacy of wisdom, his love of truth, and the deep understanding of his gentle heart will always be a beacon to the few of us who were close to him.

He who loves his son, chastises him often.
He who disciplines his son, will benefit from him.
He who spoils his son, will have wounds to bandage;
And will quake inwardly at every outcry.
Pamper your child, and he will be a terror for you.
Indulge him and he will bring you grief.

(Saint Joseph Edition of the New American Bible, Sirach 30: 1, 2, 7, 9)

Homer was a paradox to some who thought they knew him, and an outright embarrassment to others who would have had him behave in a fashion they thought would be more conducive to his station in life. Homer was a builder, a realist, and a grower of things. He had amassed a fortune, yet he enjoyed the doing more than the accumulating, and gave liberally to help people and children all over the world. Homer made millions, yet he lived an unpretentious life with his wife, Betsy, who was 20 years his junior. Together, they had a house full of children in the country.

I remember the first time I visited and was greeted by him and Betsy and a throng of bouncing, chirping children.

"Are these all yours?" I said, as I was swept along to a large picnic table in their backyard.

"Sure are," said Betsy. "Two are natural and the other seven, well, they just come to us and we love them."

"Adoption?" I asked.

Homer held a little red-haired moppet to his breast and gave her a loving squeeze. "Abandoned," he whispered. "People just can't take care of them, and they were left around, so Betsy and I, we take care of them."

The children ranged in age from 2 to 14 years old and were the happiest, healthiest, most well-behaved bunch I have ever seen. The fact that Betsy was almost blind apparently wasn't that big of a handicap working with children, for they deeply loved her and she them.

Homer had fought through Europe as a combat infantry man during World War II and had suffered three wounds. "I swore to myself," he once said, "that if God let me get back alive I was going to spend my life putting things together cause I sure as hell spent three years tearing things down."

Homer took a GI loan and turned it into a million-dollar business in the building trades industry in less than four years. In another five, he had made millions more in shipping, banking, and insurance.

Homer had few friends, but it wasn't because he didn't like people. It was partly due to his desire to live as unostentatious and simple a life as possible. Another was hatred for, as he said, stuffed shirts, status seekers, and ass-kissers. Homer also had a grudging dislike for phonies, and prided himself on being able to spot one two miles upwind in a hurricane.

One of the things I enjoyed about him though, was his ability to laugh at himself, for there was a good deal of fun in him and, on occasion, a little mischief. Homer loved showing up at board meetings wearing overalls and farmers boots, not altogether cleaned of cow manure.

If Homer had a fault, it was his overindulgence and kindness to small children and his loving obsession with his Betsy. More often than not, it was Betsy that booted him out of the house and made him go fishing. "I need good fresh fish for the children," she would say over the phone. "Don't let that man off the boat. Keep him away from my house today."

During the season, it was Homer's habit to charter the Seawitch twice a month. And I never knew until he showed up at the dock if there would be a guest or not. Sometimes he would bring a few of the older children, or maybe one or two close friends or someone he did business with. However, on one particular day in mid-September a few years back, Homer came aboard, bringing unexpected news that not only surprised me but left me a little unprepared for the events that followed.

"Am I going to upset your routine, Captain, by showing up this early?" he said leaning over the upturned engine box.

I looked up from the oil change I was laboring over to see his sunburned face. "Hell no. You should have got here a little earlier and you wouldn't have missed out on all this fun. Now I'm just about done."

"Well, like I always said, timing is everything. Better a dollar short than a day late."

I wiped my hands on a paper towel and straightened up. "What are you doing here so early?" I asked.

"Oh, I thought I'd take you and your mate to breakfast. How's that sound?"

"Fine," I said. "But Annabelle isn't due for a half hour."

"Well, that's OK. We can bring her back a muffin or a doughnut or something. Besides, maybe it's best we talk alone."

My curiosity was piquing as we walked up the ramp, but I didn't say a word until we pulled away from the dock.

"OK Homer, what's this all about? You foreclose on a widow and found out it's your long-lost sister or something?"

"No, it's worse than that," he said. "I got some relations coming aboard, and I thought I might fill you in. They're sort of a special case."

"Oh, handicapped?" I said. "We have a lot of folks who are in wheelchairs come aboard. It's no problem."

"Hell no. They're not handicapped that way. Only in the head."

"Retarded?"

"No, worse than that."

"Well, what?"

"Stupid," he said. "Just plain stupid."

"Is this your cousin that you gave the money to start a frog farm?" I asked, thinking of a conversation that we'd had earlier in the summer. "I know you had your reservations about him at the time."

"No, not Blalock. He still hasn't got all his good in the cupboard, but he's doing just fine. He paid me back ahead of time and he's got a damn good business going — sells to hotels and restaurants all over the place. Blalock is a little cracked, but he ain't stupid, if you know what I mean."

"Yeah, I guess he was smart enough to squeeze 10 grand out of you. That must've took some doing," I joked.

"That's right. It sure did, but hell, old Blalock was always a good worker. He just didn't want to work for himself until he was good and ready," Homer explained.

"Well, who you bringing down that's so important I have to be briefed?" I inquired nervously.

"My son and grandson," he answered, with a note of apology in his voice. "I never told you I was married once before because I've never been proud of the fact."

I just shook my head. "Well everyone has a skeleton in the closet, but a son? And knowing how you love kids, I don't understand?"

"You will when you meet him."

"Why?"

"Because he's a royal flaming asshole of the first water. I'll tell you all about it over breakfast."

"Does Betsy know all this?"

"Hell yes. She was the one that put this together. She's got a few ideas, and it all depends on how well things go today."

"How about your grandson? How old is he?"

"The poor rotten little shithead is 7," Homer said as we pulled into a space beside the restaurant. Let's talk about it while we eat."

Homer's story wasn't that unusual, but what was unusual was the fact that he had survived it. In 1948, Homer was well on his way to becoming a millionaire. He was a good looking young man with pleasant manners and was on the way up; he attracted the attention of the so-called 'right people at the right places.'

"Hell, I didn't know it, but I was on a sleigh ride to hell," he said. "All of a sudden I had more so-called friends than I knew what to do with. I became a member of one of these restricted country clubs and found myself up to my ass in a lifestyle that was just plain silly. All people could talk about was how much fun they were having and who was not. It was about this time that I met the daughter of my stockbroker and got married, but that didn't last too long. Just a little over a year I believe. She was a beautiful girl and her old man was a decent chap, but her mother was something else.

"She had our lives planned for us, and she figured that since I was going to be part of their family, I needed a little refinement. I mean, she said I was rough around the edges, so she began giving my wife instructions on how I should be trained. I suddenly found myself being told who I should associate with, what parties to go to, who to invite to my house, and how to dress, what kinds of car to drive, and even in some instances, who to hire and fire in my business. I told my wife that I respected her mother, but we had a life of our own. She said that her mother was only giving us good advice, and since it was free, we should be grateful."

"Well I can see why you got out of that," I said. "What happened to your wife?"

Homer sat down his coffee cup. "Well, let me finish. I guess the straw that broke the camel's back came when my bookkeeper pulled me aside and showed me the cost of all that friendly family advice. Why, my wife and her mother spent almost $100,000, all my money, in just a little over four months sanding down my rough edges.

"Those two women took a damn nice home that I liked, threw out a lot of decent furniture and filled it with a lot of overpriced shit that made the place look like a cold museum. I know this sounds a bit far out, but it gets worse.

"I had an invitation to sit at the same table with Harry Truman during this American Legion thing and when Vicky — that was my wife's name — found out, she screamed that she had nothing to wear. I asked her about the $7,000 that she has spent on a shopping trip in Boston with her mother a few weeks back, and she went into a rage. Said that I shouldn't care what she spent on herself because it was all for me, and I had no right checking up on her. Well, that was it. I told her there would be no new dress, and she stomped out of the house and went home to mother. I didn't know it at the time, but she was eight weeks pregnant with my son."

"Did you try to patch things up?"

"Hell, I didn't have time. Next thing I knew, her mother got this judge to annul the marriage, and I got nailed with all this court shit that cost me another bundle. Vicky never told her mother that she was pregnant until after the annulment. Boy, let me tell you, did the shit ever hit the fan! Her mother had arranged to take Vicky up to Canada to get an abortion when I found out and called her father. Well, the old man wasn't going to see his grandchild destroyed, so he stopped it. Vicky went off someplace in California and had the child, named Roger. I didn't get to see the kid until he was 6 months, and I had to go to court to do that." Homer explained.

"What happened to Vicky?"

"Her father died when the boy was 2 years old, and she was left with a lot of money. Her and the old lady went to Europe, and she got in with this what you call jet-set crowd. Married this guy from one of those little Eastern European countries that the Russians overran in '45. His name was Prince Ugon Von Nosebleed or some damn thing. She had Roger's name changed to Dolph Von whatever, but he changed it when he got older to Lewis."

"Maybe he wanted to please you?"

"Don't fool yourself, boy. He found out his old man had a few bucks, and he was just covering all bets. As I was saying, Vicky found out this Von whatever didn't have a dime that was his own, so she ditched him. And she's been through five husbands at last count and at least two face lifts that I know of. I saw a picture of her awhile back, and she had the skin stretched so tight around her mouth she looked like a codfish."

"Why don't you tell me about Roger," I said. "I can't understand why you're so dead-set against him."

Homer looked somewhat sullen and lowered his head. "Roger's my son," he began, "but I have to admit to you that I have never known a more status-seeking, social-climbing, pompous ass in all my life. I tried to get near him when he was growing up, but his mother made sure that I didn't. She stuck the boy in some damn English prep school when he was just a kid, 7 or 8, and left him. I went over a few times, but it just wasn't enough. The boy never had love growing up, only rules and regulations. Vicky and her old lady did everything to poison that kid against me. I used to write to him, but he resented me — told me I was a traitor to my class. I didn't say much to him, as I figured in time he would want to hear my side of the story."

"Did you ever tell him?"

"Sure, I went up to Dartmouth just as he was finishing up, and we had a talk. He listened, and he was very polite, but it was all an act."

"What makes you think that? At least he listened."

"Well every now and then, I gave their medical school a little money, and I know a few of the boys that teach up there. I guess someone told him how much they appreciated my gifts over the years, and as how he was my son, it was nice to have him at school. Well, I have to hand it to the kid, he learned to cash in on my name damn fast.".

"I got a call from a friend, and he said that I should have a little talk with Roger, as he was fast becoming an overindulgent, insufferable little snob who used my name to buy a few people around. I called the school president up and told him I had nothing to do with him being up there, and his tuition was being paid for by a trust fund set up by his grandfather. I also said that I would be more than pleased if they threw his ass out. Well, that's why he was so polite when I went up there; he'd had his ass renamed and was afraid that I would use my influence to get him bounced. His social status and standing with his group of friends was in jeopardy and heaven knows he wouldn't do anything to lose his place in the pecking order," he continued.

"How about your grandson? Do you try to see him?" I questioned.

Homer gave me his 'do bears shit in the woods look' and shook his head. "Hell yes! I go see the little prick. He's one of those kids that keeps his parents in turmoil. He's spoiled rotten to the core and a selfish little bastard that screams if he doesn't get his way every minute," he demonstrated.

"Do they do anything about it?" I asked.

"Nope, they just ignore him most of the time. From what I understand, the kid gets sent to one or two head doctors two or three times a week. He's what people used to refer to as a problem child and that's why I've unloaded all this on you today. You and Annabelle are going to earn your keep. He's a hyperactive boy, and we'll all have to watch him." Homer justified.

"Thanks," I said. "What in the hell did I do that got me on Betsy's shit list?"

"Nothing, but Betsy has a plan and she wants a crack at that kid," he answered.

"Cripes! I can't believe it! As if she didn't have enough to do. Would you want him there?" I shouted.

"You know damn well I would. There's nothing that a lot of love and a swift kick in the ass wouldn't cure as far as that kid is concerned," Homer pushed himself away from the table and stared at the ceiling for a moment. "Did I ever tell you about my old man?" he said with a note of mellowness in his voice.

"Not much, only something about him being a hobo for a while or something like that," I replied.

Homer shook his head again and whistled through his teeth. "Boy, he was a real pisser," he said smiling. "He's been dead 40 years, but I still love him. Remind me to tell you about him sometime."

During the ride back to the harbor, Homer didn't say a word until a pale green Rolls convertible with white top pulled ahead of us just as we were about to turn onto Route 6A.

"That's the asshole now," he said pointing at the Rolls. "You got any idea how much that damn car cost?"

"No," I said. "You begrudge him a nice car?"

"Hell no! I don't begrudge anyone anything as long as they earn it, but he didn't earn it. As a matter of fact, he hasn't worked a day since he left college," he explained.

I watched the Rolls turn onto Millway and head for the harbor. "Well, someone is supporting him in style. Is it your ex-wife?" I asked.

"No, I told you, he's no dummy. He married into one of those Newport families, and his wife takes care of him. She isn't a bad person either. I liked her the first time I met her, and I still don't know what the hell she sees in him, but she loves him and he's smart enough to know where his bread is buttered," Homer stated.

"Does he love her, or does he just stick around because of the money?" I inquired.

"I'm not sure, but I think he loves her," he sighed, his arms up in the air.

We were interrupted when I rounded the corner just in time to see the Rolls pull into a parking space beside the booking booth.

"Let me off here," said Homer. "I'll go greet the bastards and bring them down to the boat. That way you'll have time to brief Annabelle about the kid."

As Homer went to greet Roger and his grandson, I told Annabelle the boy may be difficult.

Following him with her eyes, Annabelle said, "I wouldn't worry, Capt." She tipped a container of orange juice to her lips. "Mr. Lewis has brought lots of kids down and we never had a bit of trouble. They were all well-behaved."

"This isn't one of those kids," I said. "This kid is hyperactive, and you're going to have to be on your toes."

Annabelle finished her juice. "Well, he's just one kid. I mean, how much trouble can he be?"

I was about to answer when a shower of gravel splattered in the cockpit and on the deck. Annabelle let out a scream as I looked up at the bulkhead to see a white, chubby face disappear.

"Osmond, you'll get your hands dirty," said a voice from the direction of the ramp.

"Oh my God!" said Annabelle. "Was that—"

"I'm afraid so. Now what were you telling me a second ago?"

"I was going to ..." Annabelle's voice trailed off as another blizzard of gravel rained down at the foot of the ramp. "Oh shit!"

"Osmond, your hands," said Roger, the boy shooting passed him at the bottom of the ramp and running full-speed down the length of our dock.

"Any damage?" asked Homer, as he and his son walked up to the transom.

"No, I don't think so," I said. "Annabelle and I were standing under the top, and thank heavens no one was standing at the foot of the ramp."

Homer nodded. "Well, thank God for small favors," he said looking in the direction his grandson had run. "Bob, this is my son, Roger Lewis."

I offered my hand noticing that Roger seemed to be staring at a point about one inch above my head, and my hand was greeted with a set of car keys that dangled from his.

"Cook has prepared a hamper. You'll find it in the trunk of the Rolls. Would you bring it down please?"

"Certainly," I said taking the keys and flipping them to Annabelle. "You'll find it in the green car beside Homer's Ford."

Annabelle took the keys and curtsied, rolling her eyes heavenwards and fluttering her eyelashes.

"Amusing," said Roger, now looking directly at me. "What does one call you?"

"Captain will do just fine," I said very slowly, looking directly in his eyes.

Homer stared at the dock. "I'll go find Osmond," he said smiling.

Roger looked about the boat, then took a seat in the fighting chair.

"Osmond and I are not interested in blood sports," he said, opening a copy of Gentlemen's Quarterly. "Dr. Ramsey says no child should be subjected to the wanton slaughtering of innocent creatures for the sake of sport."

"Are you and your son vegetarians, Mr. Lewis?"

"No, we're not."

"Do you eat seafood at all?"

"On occasion."

"Well, we don't kill for the hell of it on this boat. It's either eaten or sold. Otherwise, we let it swim."

Roger busied himself with Gentlemen's Quarterly, and I took the wicker hamper that Annabelle sat down on the bait tank.

"Oh, by the way," he said looking up from his magazine. "Is this stink pot safe?"

Annabelle's face bleached beneath her suntan. No one, but no one called her boat a stink pot, even if it was a common term used by the sailboat community to describe power boats.

"I don't think so," I said. "It has two major components involved in its operation that are totally unpredictable and have been known to become violent and dangerous when provoked. They're its captain and its first mate. You must remember you're dealing with simple, uneducated people who are very intolerant of any rudeness or bullshit."

Roger's smug expression turned into genuine laughter that was perfectly refreshing. "Oh well, I see, I'll certainly take it under advisement," he said.

Annabelle grabbed the opportunity to introduce herself and return the keys to Roger.

"Are you in school?" he asked.

"I'm at Mount Holyoke. I graduate next year."

"Oh my! My wife's a Mount Holyoke alumna. I used to drive down from Dartmouth on weekends. I know the area quite well."

Annabelle smiled at Roger as her apprehension disappeared and common ground was struck.

"What does your family do?" he probed.

"My dad works for the power company and my mom's a nurse," she answered.

Roger's face clouded for an instant. "Oh, how very nice," he said. "They must be quite pleased with you?"

Annabelle detected the change and went back on the defensive. "Yes, they are. They're giving up a lot to put me through school, and I do my best for them."

"Well, I'm sure you do," Roger said turning back to his magazine.

The ride into the bay was uneventful for Annabelle and me, while Homer made small talk with Roger, who held Osmond throttled by his collar.

"Do you know what we call a person like that at school?" Annabelle said looking back at our guest. "A terminal preppie. I can't stand anyone who looks down at people the way that guy does. I know kids like that and they're disgusting."

"You should feel sorry for them."

"I do, but I just can't stand to be around them."

Osmond broke away from his father and started screaming, "Don't hold me! I got to go to the bathroom! I gotta go to the bathroom!"

Annabelle ran aft and took Osmond by the hand. "I'll show you how to use the head," she said. "Come with me."

Osmond screamed and broke away. "No, I don't like you! I hate you!"

"Now, Osmond," said Roger. "Remember what Dr. Ramsey said, we must not be impolite. Let Annabelle show you how to use the bathroom."

"No, I'll pee in my pants."

"Very well, Osmond. If you do, you'll feel very uncomfortable for the rest of the day," Roger explained calmly.

"I don't care. I hate you."

"All right, Osmond. Do as you wish."

Homer's face went to ash as he looked at his grandson, then at this son. "I'll take you to the head," he said offering his hand to the boy.

Osmond cocked his head back and spit at his grandfather, then ran toward the cabin. "I hate you!" he screamed. "I hate you!"

"Pay no attention to Osmond," explained his father. "He often behaves in this fashion when subjected to unfamiliar people or new surroundings. Dr. Rasseu said it's a normal reaction and nothing to be alarmed about."

Annabelle followed Osmond into the cabin and returned to report that he had went into the head and shut the door behind him.

"My God!" Homer said joining me at the wheel. "Do you think I would ever put up with that behavior? That little bastard's got everyone scared to death and buffaloed."

"I feel sorry for both of them" I said. "There's nothing wrong with that kid that couldn't be taken care of in short order, and as a matter of fact, Roger's not a bad person either once you get past all the crap."

"Well, you must see something in him that I don't."

"I did, and it didn't take me long to find out," I said.

"How in the hell did you do that? He's never been anything but a polite snob around me," he inquired.

"I told him, in so many words, that if he didn't cut the BS, Annabelle and I would rearrange his anatomy."

Homer's face showed doubt. "You're kidding?" he said, a questioning note in his voice.

"No, I don't think so. I believe he's a human being, even after all you've told me. I think if you ever got past all the garbage he puts up in front of him, you'll find that you son isn't what he pretends to be."

Homer shrugged his shoulders and managed a smile. "Well that's nice to know," he said, making his way back to the fighting chair.

Annabelle started into the cabin just as Osmond pushed past her onto the deck. "Go below and see what that filthy little Klingon has done," she muttered, taking the wheel from me.

I ducked below to see that several tackle boxes had been emptied in a pile and the contents of cabinets and drawers were in a tangled, hopeless mess.

"My God! He was only down there three minutes," she cried as I started past her. "That will take me hours to straighten out."

Roger and his father inspected the mess while I confronted Osmond.

"I didn't do anything!" he screamed at the top of his lungs. "Leave me alone! I hate you!"

I hadn't said a word to the boy, but I gave him a look that sent him flying for the cabin and the protection of his father. However, Annabelle stole the moment and stuck her bare foot into Osmond's path and sent the boy sprawling in a heap beside the engine box.

"Osmond, you must be more careful. You shouldn't run so," she said, smiling sweetly at the child.

Osmond was speechless, but not for long. He cocked his head and filled his lungs for a mighty yell, which was preempted by a healthy squirt from our wash down hose.

"Oh my! Now how did that get turned on?" Annabelle said, flipping the switch off.

Osmond sat stunned and stared with a glazed-over face at Annabelle.

"Come with me," she said, pulling the boy to his feet. "Let's get you dried off now."

Osmond followed her to the cabin without saying a word.

"I'm sorry, Captain," Roger said, coming on deck. "I'm sure there's no damage to the equipment. I'll see that Annabelle is paid for the extra work. We all must remember that Osmond is a child in his experimental and informative years. Dr. Ramsey and Dr. Van Dorn both agree that nothing should be done to stifle Osmond's curiosity, and as a matter of fact, it should be indulged whenever possible."

Homer looked at his son and shook his head. "I've never heard of such cow shit in all my life. You have a half-brother and half-sister and there's seven other beautiful children at my home, and not one of them has behaved that way in their lives. I think both of your doctors are feeding you a bunch of high-priced crap."

"I disagree," Roger said. "Why, Rasseu and VanDorn are the top people in their field, and I'm sure most of Newport would agree with me."

"Most of Newport?"

"That's correct."

"Good Lord! May God have mercy on the lot of you."

Roger turned to see Osmond back on deck.

"Osmond. You've gotten yourself wet," Homer said irritated.

"Oh, it wasn't Osmond fault. He had a little accident," explained Annabelle. "But everything is just fine now."

Osmond looked at his father, then up to Annabelle, who was drying his head with a towel.

"Osmond is going to help me straighten out a few things below. Aren't you Osmond?"

The boy looked at Annabelle a second time and shook his head to the affirmative. "I'll help," he said.

Roger blinked at me. "My! He's certainly taken with her. That's unusual for Osmond. Very seldom does he say yes to anything."

Roger glanced at his father, who was watching his grandson follow Annabelle's directions.

"I'll certainly mention this to Dr. Ramsey. He's never behaved like this before," Roger said flabbergasted.

Several schools of mackerel were pushing along the surface as I reduced speed, pulled the throttle into neutral, and killed the engine.

"I prefer to watch," said Roger addressing his father. "I told the captain that Osmond and I are not really into blood sports."

Homer took a spinning rod with two feathered jigs and flipped it into a school. "Nothing is wasted," he said jigging the rod and hooking a fish. "Betsy and I don't like a lot of chemicals in our food, and we and the children love fresh fish."

Roger watched as the two shimmering fish were swung over the side.

"They have strips like a tiger, don't they?" Homer persisted.

Just then, Annabelle and Osmond were about to go into the cabin, Homer held the fish up for Osmond to see. "That's right. I call 'em tiger fish."

Osmond was amazed and gaped at the fish with a face filled with wonder. "I want to do one," he said.

"All right. I'll teach your father, and Annabelle can teach you. Okay?"

"But I've never fished before," Roger explained.

Homer laughed at his son. "There's a hell of a lot of things you haven't done," he said, handing Roger the spinning rod.

Within 10 minutes, Roger was on his own and obviously enjoying himself, despite his preconceptions. Homer stood by and unhooked fish as Roger swung them aboard.

"I must admit, they do put up a struggle," he said. "I can't imagine what something like a marlin could do."

Annabelle and Osmond had taken one rod and a bucket and were sitting together on the bow. Osmond watched Annabelle's every move and punctuated her instructions every now and then with a giggle or a burst of laughter.

"I don't think I have ever seen that child so engrossed," remarked Roger to his father. "That girl certainly has a way with him."

Homer watched his grandson for a moment and turned to me. "I think we have enough of these," he said. "Let's go for some blues."

I started the engine and had everyone pull in lines.

"How did she do it?" he asked as I pushed the throttle up to cruise.

"I'm not saying a word, but you can guess," I said.

Homer turned to Annabelle as Osmond went aft to show his father his bucket of mackerel.

"How did you do it so quick?" he asked looking after his grandson.

"I have two little brothers at home," answered Annabelle. "I know how to handle kids."

"I didn't ask you about your little brothers, young lady. I asked you about that little bastard. How did you get him to behave so fast?"

Annabelle looked at me, and then at Homer. "I sprawled him on the deck, stuck a hose in his face, and when I took him below I told him if he told I would reach down his throat and rip his heart out and feed it to the sharks."

Homer laughed. "Well, I see you and Betsy are of the same school."

"I hope you're not mad, Mr. Lewis, but that kid needed it, and I really didn't hurt him that much."

Homer put his hand on Annabelle's shoulder. "Oh, I don't think you hurt the child, but you just may have helped save his life."

"I don't understand," Annabelle questioned as Homer went to talk with his son.

"I hope Mr. Lewis doesn't tell him what I did," Annabelle said to me.

"Don't worry," I said. "You only did what someone should have been doing right along."

On the other side of the deck, Roger shook his head and pointed at his father. "That is most definitely out of the question. Why Dr. Ramsey would never allow it and I know Jane wouldn't hear of it either. What you're proposing could have a disastrous effect on Osmond. You know he isn't like other children."

Homer pointed in the direction of his grandson, who was helping Annabelle spool on a coil of wire.

"Roger, I want you to listen to me like you've never listened before. I know you don't give a shit about me, but it isn't Osmond that's different. It's you and your wife; the two of you are killing that child."

"Why that's ridiculous, Homer. We give Osmond everything."

Homer spun the fighting chair around that Roger was sitting in and faced him forward. "Look what's happening," he said. "Pay attention."

The child and the girl sat cross-legged facing on another, he with a roll of wire and she with a reel.

"Those are funny words," he said giggling into her face. "I can't sing those."

"Oh yes you can," she said spinning the reel and laughing. "There once was a fish."

"There once was a fish."

"Whose name was McNish."

"Whose name was Mc..."

Roger watched them for a time. "I've never heard my child sing before," he said to his father. "What would Jane say?"

"She already has," Homer said looking at his son. "She came to Betsy two weeks ago. It's all up to you."

"But it's complicated. I'll have to explain. I'll have ..." Roger broke off.

"You'll have to nothing," said Homer. "Jane picked up Betsy this morning on her way down with Osmond's things. They're going to meet us at the dock."

Roger looked at Homer for the last time and his father for the first time.

"Tell me about the marlin?" he requested.

My mate, Annabelle

Cleveland

Miranda's wedding present and me in my younger days

The famous Cleveland Tuna

Dolphins swimming up beside the boat

Catching a polluck

A view of the harbor from the dock

Cleveland steering the boat

The Seawitch heading out of the harbor

Marinda at rest

My Cesna C150

SEP

My friend, Homer, on a fishing charter trip

Captain Lobster's boat

A full view of the Seawitch out at sea

Heading into harbor while a storm rolls into the Cape

Part of the Firehouse Fire, Suds Sudolski

My mates and me in my younger days

Captain and the kid

Customer with fish

Lt. Commander, Admiral, Captain, and Cleveland

Chapter 9

Fish Spotter

The sun had not quite reached the edge of the tree line at the far end of the runway when I parked my pickup beside the hanger. I looked around for Old Jim, as his ancient brown Chevy was in its accustomed place. However, there wasn't a sign of movement anywhere except for a lone sea gull that was entering a right downwind for runway 18.

'Must have gone for coffee with someone,' I thought, stretching my legs and pushing the truck door shut. The padlock between the hanger doors had been snapped free and Worcester, Old Jim's gray and overfed cat, sat patiently waiting to be let in.

"Good morning, you old hitchhiker," I said scratching him between the ears.

The cat had gotten his name because as a kitten he had stowed away beneath the seat of a Cessna 140 that a student pilot, a girl of 18, had flown to Worcester. It was summer, and she had a habit of flying in her bare feet and wasn't aware of her passenger until the return flight was almost over. She was about a mile from our field and about to let down to pattern altitude when this little fur ball rubbed between her ankles, triggering the tomcat spin, a non-approved flight maneuver that those who witnessed doubt could ever be duplicated again. Worcester had become a legend in his own time, as well as a pain in the backside to unsuspecting pilots. The cat had logged hundreds of hours of flight time and, somehow, Lady Luck and the unique aluminum collar that Jim had fashioned for him always got him home.

I pushed the hanger door aside to find my Cessna gone, but I didn't have to wait more than a minute before I heard the sound of my airplane over the field.

Old Jim gave me a thumbs-up as he rolled up on the grass and killed the engine. "She's running tip top," he said popping open the aluminum door. "I finished the annual last night and you're all set for another season, Capt."

I smiled gratefully and thanked the man. One of the things I had learned was to love, trust, and obey one's mechanic, especially when one flies a single-engine aircraft over the sea at low altitudes.

"See anything?" I asked.

"Not much. Just a bunch of birds on the flats in front of your harbor, and it looks like someone spilled a lot of oil on the water northwest of the shoals."

"Any boats around it?"

"Nope, Capt. And no birds either."

"Well, that's where I'll start looking," I said.

Earlier that week I had explained to Jim that it was all we could do to catch a half dozen fish a trip and that every charter and private boat from Sandwich to Provincetown was having the same problem. Our sport fishing season had started off slow, then went dead, along with the weather, which for the last four days had kept every boat bottled up in port. I, along with most other captains, had spent long hours on the phone canceling and postponing trips with hopes that things would soon improve. And this morning was the first in over 10 days that was clear and sunny with no wind.

"You gonna fish today?" Jim asked, shading his eyes and looking in the direction of the horizon.

"No, I don't have a trip," I said. "They rebooked for another day. Hey, where is that flea-bitten friend of yours?"

"Damn good-for-nothing cat's been gone for a week," Jim stated flatly.

"Well, he's back now," I said expecting Jim to relax the scowl on his face. "I just let him in."

Jim's expression remained frozen. "You know what that flea-bitten son-of-a-bitch did last week?"

"No," I said slowly. "What did he do this time?"

"Well you know Dave Bishop, who flies for Delta?"

"Yes," I nodded.

"Well, he got in the back of Dave's Cessna and went to Boston. Dave didn't have time to give him to someone heading back here, so he took him aboard his 737, and they went to Miami and spent the night. Then off to Chicago and to God knows where! Anyway, George Fountain, who flies for Eastern, dropped him off his way home last Wednesday."

"That's nothing new," I said. "Why are you upset?"

"Upset! Hell, I'm not upset. I'm jealous. That bastard got first class. How would you like to ride around the country free of charge, getting great meals, and have young, beautiful stews fussing over you?"

"I get your point," I said, beginning to feel a little envious of the cat.

"Go find fish," Jim ordered walking away. "I'll see you when you get back."

I checked the windsock for motion, found nothing, and then buckled myself into the Cessna. At 1,000 feet I leveled off, pulled the power back to 70 percent, and set the trim so that she all but flew herself. Thin jellyrolls of ground fog queued up in rows along the coast and mirrored back twins in the still water. Beneath my port wing, two small outboards cut white Vs as the headed east toward Orleans, while directly ahead a gray lobster boat turned his stern to the sun, lining up with a long, jagged row of white pots. I dipped the nose a bit and waggled my wings in salute as I flew seaward.

Flying was not only a relaxing and enjoyable thing for me, it was also one of the most financially smart things I had ever been involved in as a fisherman. In most cases, a few gallons of aviation fuel and less than an hour flight time each morning would save endless hours of searching and hundreds of gallons of boat fuel each week. As a matter of record, the money saved on boat fuel paid for the airplane in three and a half seasons.

Provincetown inked itself into the picture ahead as I scanned the instrument panel before letting down to a spotting altitude of 600 feet. Locating fish from the air was easy, providing the weather cooperated and the surface winds were less than 12 knots. And this morning, the conditions were ideal. The sea was flat, and the water was so clear that in some places the bottom could be seen in 15 fathoms. I flew a zigzag course, making slow turns every half-mile or so and not spotting a thing. I was sure I had covered the area that Jim had talked about earlier and was about to fly shoreward when the dark bluish-green water beneath my starboard wing flashed silver. I made a shallow turn to the left and was about to level off when one of the most amazing sights I had ever seen filled the windscreen before me.

Thousands of giant striped bass clouded and sparkled a dull silver in the sea for miles ahead. Thank God for the automatic responses that kept me flying the airplane because my brain was having trouble comprehending the sight that was unfolding before me. I had seen schools of fish before and had listed to stories from other pilots and captains, but nothing I had ever heard of or seen came close to matching what I was now flying over.

I pushed the throttle to full power and climbed up an additional 300 feet or so to get a better perspective of this body of fish, which shimmered and snake-danced in ribbons underneath me. The school was almost a quarter mile wide and stretched along a southeasterly course for two and a half miles. Beneath the silver surface of fish, which was only the tip of the iceberg, legions of dark bullet shapes marched in unison, canopied by their brothers.

I circled the school twice more, then bee-lined a little less than full throttle back to the strip, feeling something akin to a prospector who had just hit the mother lode.

"Hey Capt. There's some people from the motel down on the boat," Annabelle announced when I got back to Barnstable. "They may want to go out today."

I nodded OK and went and introduced myself to four vacationing stockbrokers from New York City.

"What's the chances of getting bass?" asked the spokesperson of the group.

"Good," I said giving them my best smile.

"We've been hearing that the fishing has been lousy and no one's bringing anything in."

"That's right," I said. "It has been, but you'll do good."

"Can you guarantee it?"

"No, I can't," I answered, still grinning for all I was worth.

"Do we have to pay if we don't catch anything?" he asked.

"Sure," I said. "Unless you want to go for double or nothing.'

"How does that work?"

"Simple. If you don't catch fish, you don't pay. If you do, you pay double."

"Just a minute," he said herding his group into a small circle at the end of my dock. "Let us decide."

Annabelle gave me a what-in-the-hell-are-you-doing look while I stared off into space, still holding my grin.

"OK, we'll take the bet," the gentleman said. "After all, we're gamblers anyway."

Later that night, after off-loading over 800 pounds of bass and having dinner with my four stockbrokers and Annabelle, I felt that somehow I owed a debt to the Wright brothers and to that dusty old curmudgeon who fussed over my Cessna.

Chapter 10

Bleep, Bleep

Dear reader, the following short story is a work of fiction based on a series of events that happened over the course of a nine-day period a few years back. I have had to take a lot of poetic license in describing this series of events, as a great deal for the information pertaining to them came to me third- and fourth-hand. However, friends, fear not. It's not how it happened that's so important; it's what happened that counts. And what happened is something that most of those involved would deny ever happened at all.

Day 1

The following is a citizens' band radio conversation between Captain Lobster and Captain Short, a lobster fisherman from another harbor.

Captain Lobster: *Well, Captain Short, you old pirate; I bet you got that scow filled to the **gunnels** by now.*

Captain Short: *Hell no, Captain. I'd never want to do that.*

Captain Lobster: *And just why the hell not? You never showed them critters any mercy before. Why all of a sudden are you some damn kind of conservationist or something?*

Captain Short: *Yep, that's right, Captain. I'm only filling this slab up to the* **scuppers** *and no more. I just don't wanna be bothered handling the pesky things.*

Captain Lobster: *Then you must have a good reason.*

Captain Short: *Yep, sure do.*

Captain Lobster: *What is it?*

Captain Short: *Well, me and the missus wouldn't wanna lose out all the fun down at the welfare office. You start making money, and you can't go down there and see all your friends.*

Captain Lobster: *Well, I get your point, Captain. You suppose they got room for me?*

Captain Short: *Don't know, Captain. I think you make too much money.*

Captain Lobster: *I'll tell you, Captain Short, if they knew what I made they'd have a brass band march me up to the head of line.*

Captain Short: *Well Captain, you might as well come on ...*

Captain Short's voice trailed off and there was a moment of dead air on the radio.

Captain Lobster: *Well, did you fall overboard?*

Captain Short: *Standby, Captain. We just found something driftin' in the* **pots***. We're going to bring it aboard.*

A full five minutes passed before Captain Lobster tired of waiting and keyed the mic.

Captain Lobster: *Well short, what did you find?*

Captain Short: *I-I don't know, Captain. I don't know what the hell it is!*

Captain Lobster: *Well, what's it look like?*

Captain Short: *I'm not sure. Looks like a can or something.*

Captain Lobster: *Ain't no depth charge or mine is it? You could get blown up.*

Captain Short: *I just don't know. It seems too light for that. It damn near don't weight nothing.*

Captain Lobster: *Well, how big is it?*

Captain Short: *I suppose it's four feet or so at its tallest, and two or three feet at the round front part.*

Captain Lobster: *I bet it's a navigational buoy broke away from some harbor up the coast.*

Captain Short: *Don't think so.*

Captain Lobster: *Why?*

Captain Short: *Cause they ain't no place to hook a line to it. If it was a buoy there'd be a place to hook a line or chain or something, but there ain't.*

Captain Lobster didn't answer right away, as he was busy hauling a pot.

Captain Lobster: *How did you get it aboard?*

Captain Short: *I lassoed it 'round the skinny part in the middle, right between the two windows.*

Captain Lobster: *Windows! You didn't say it had windows.*

Captain Short: *Well, I don't recollect you askin'.*

Captain Lobster: *Sounds like you got a fallen satellite or something. You know how the government is always saying that they're falling out of the sky.*

Captain Short: *Maybe, but it ain't burned or anything.*

Captain Lobster: *What's it made of?*

Captain Short: *Some kind of metal, I guess. It's got a nice shine to it.*

Captain Lobster: *Is there any writing or numbers on it, Short?*

Captain Short: *Yep. It's got a whole bunch of letters and numbers, but it doesn't make a lot of sense. I'll go aft and take a real long look at it and call you back.*

The better part of 10 minutes slipped by before Captain Short came back on the radio.

Captain Short: *I'll be damned, Captain Lobster if that ain't the damnedest thing I ever did see.*

Captain Lobster: *Well, what is it, Short? What did you find out?*

Captain Short: *I don't know what it is, but I found out it's got these queer lights inside, all red and green and the like. Kind of pretty in there.*

Captain Lobster: *Sounds like you found one of them things we saw in that Star Wars movie. You remember? It looked like a mailbox with feet. The mate said it's an R2-D2 — a robot or something.*

Captain Short: *This ain't got feet, but it does make a noise. I tapped it a few times with the hammer and it went 'bleep'.*

Captain Lobster: *Went what?*

Captain Short: *'Bleep', damn it.*

Captain Lobster: *'Bleep'?*

Captain Short: *Damn you, Lobster! Clean the shit outta your ears. 'Bleep', damn it. I said it went 'bleep'!*

Day 2

A red jeep with the words 'Town Harbormaster' lettered on its side pulled into Captain Short's driveway. Captain Short leans against his pickup truck smoking his pipe.

"Mornin' Robert," he said to the man as he slid from behind the driver's seat.

"Morning Henry. What the hell's all this business I'm hearing about, you find some kind of bomb or something?"

"Yep, but it ain't blown up."

"Well, what is it Henry? Do you know?"

Henry banged his pipe empty on the side of his pickup and then started walking toward his work shed. "If I knew that, what would I have called you up for?"

The harbormaster didn't say a word and fell into step behind Henry.

"You know all about buoys and things for navigation, don't you?" Henry asked.

"I know some," he said as Henry stops long enough to swing wide his shed doors.

"Then tell me, what the hell is this damn thing."

The harbormaster's eyes fell on the object that now rested on two sawhorses in the subdued light of the shed. "Why it's ah ... why it's ah ... Damn, Henry! I don't know what the hell that is. I never seen anything like that in my life. Is that lights in it?"

Henry shook his head. "Yep. Me and the missus and the neighbors had a grand time watchin' it last night. Sure is a puzzler."

The harbormaster circled the object and rubbed his hand on the smooth metal surface. "Boy, Henry, you sure found something."

"Yep, guess I did."

"Why don't you shake it?"

"Why, I don't want to upset it. It may be some kind of explosive device or a time bomb. I mean who the hell knows."

Henry walked up to the device and wobbled it back and forth between the two sawhorses, causing the device to emit a loud metal 'bleep'. The already apprehensive and now startled harbormaster skipped back through the shed door into the daylight.

"That damn thing may be dangerous, Henry. You best keep away. I'm going to get the Coast Guard."

"Well, tell 'em it goes 'bleep,'" added Henry as the harbormaster's jeep rumbled out of his driveway.

Within the hour, the sound of another vehicle pulling into his yard sent him out his kitchen door, coffee cup in hand. "It's the Coast Guard," Henry said back through the door.

"Oh, how nice," replied a pleasant voice from in the kitchen. "Tell them when they're through they can come in for coffee and turnovers, dear."

When the men were done, they visited Mrs. Short in the kitchen.

"Are you sure you can't hold just one more, young man?" said Mrs. Short to one of the handsome young Coast Guardsmen who'd just finished his second cup of coffee and third peach turnover.

"No thank you, ma'am. That was wonderful. We've already stayed a little too long."

The other young man smiled up at Mrs. Short. "I'm stuffed," he said.

Henry pushed himself away from the table and fired up his second pipe of the day. "Well boys, if you've never seen anything like it, maybe you better call the Navy or some of them government people."

"Our commander will know what to do, sir. I'm sure he'll be able to find out what it is and who owns it," answered one of the young men.

"Yes, sir," said the other confidently. "We'll find out what it is and let you know as soon as possible."

Day 3

Henry returned home after pulling his pots and got the following report from Mrs. Short.

At about 10:30 that morning, two uniformed men wearing a lot of ribbons rang the doorbell and asked Mrs. Short if they could go out in the shed.

"They were only here a minute," she told Henry. "They went into the shed and when they came out, they had a foot race to see who could get to the car first. Why they didn't even say goodbye or stay for coffee."

Day 4

Henry was about to step into his pickup and drive to the harbor when a large chauffeur-driven sedan pulled up blocking his driveway. Two men in dark suits and another man in uniform got out and walked up to him. They were about to introduce themselves when Henry pointed to the shed.

"What you want is in there," he said.

They open the shed door and then freeze in their tracks.

"Oh my aching ass," said the man in uniform.

"Oh shit," said one of the other men.

The third man stood speechless with his mouth open.

Henry spent the next hour telling the three men how he found the thing and demanded to know what it is and who lost it.

"I can't tell you what it is because if I do, I'll break the law," said one of the men in a suit. "But I will tell you this." He turned and glared angrily at his companions. "The guys behind the eight ball that are responsible for this are going to have their asses on a meat hook."

"Well, we won't have any of that," said Henry. "Ain't nobody going to get punished for losing that funny-lookin' can. Why there ain't a damn place to tie it down! No wonder it fell in the water. Anyways, folks around here love and respect their Coast Guard and work hand-in-hand with them year in and year out. Besides those boys are like family in this town."

"It wasn't the Coast Guard who lost it," one of the uniformed men said.

"Well I don't give a damn who lost it. I found it and you ain't getting it back till I find out what all this business is about."

Day 5

Early morning radio traffic between Captain Lobster, Captain Indian, and the Seawitch.

Captain Indian: *Well boys, looks like we got company this morning.*

I was about to make a remark when three large helicopters in formation came thundering in the Sandy Neck and passed directly over us at less than 500 feet.

Seawitch: *Helicopters?*

Captain Lobster: *Just keep coming, Seawitch. You and the Indian will see us as soon as you get a couple of miles north of the bell.*

I put the Seawitch on a 30-degree heading that paralleled Captain Indian, who was 500 yards on our port, and brought my engine RPMs down 200, which kept us even. The three helicopters appeared to reduce their speed and were now in a line abreast at right angles to us, flying less than 100 feet above the water.

Seawitch: *What do you suppose those guys are doing?*

Captain Lobster: *Maybe war games or something. Or maybe they're expecting an invasion from New Hampshire. You know our lobster fishermen and their lobster fishermen are always going at it. I guess armed hostilities have broken out.*

Seawitch: *Hell, that ain't nothing new. Those boys have been feuding longer than the Hatfields and the McCoys.*

Captain Indian: *Well then it can only be one other thing.*

Seawitch: *What's that?*

Captain Indian: *I think someone told them that Captain Lobster was in the pot business, and it's a drug raid.*

Captain Lobster: *Oh Lord! I'm doomed. They've found me out.*

The helicopters made a wide sweep to the southwest, then again to the north, and disappeared out to sea.

Captain Indian: *Cripes! Those look like ships of some kind out there. What in the hell are they?*

Captain Lobster: *Like I told you, when you get out here where I'm at, you'll find out.*

In a few minutes, the outline of two ships began to take shape as we closed in.

Captain Indian: *Why, those look like destroyers!*

Captain Lobster: *Yep. Them's destroyers.*

Captain Indian: *What in heaven do you suppose they're doing here?*

Captain Lobster: *I don't know. Why don't you go and ask them? Tell them you're a tax payer and you want to know just what they're doing here and demand to know how they're spending our money today.*

Captain Indian: *Shit! I spent half a lifetime in the service and I ain't ever going near one of those buckets again.*

Through the binoculars, I could see that the destroyers were dead in the water and drifting. Since they were on my course line to where I would be fishing for the morning, I thought it would be interesting to have a closer look at the Navy. After all, it just wasn't an everyday occurrence to have destroyers come into the bay. Annabelle and two young ladies, who were part of our party for the trip, were delighted at the prospect.

"Can we go up on the bow?" they asked. "We want to take pictures."

I thought how odd it was that the three girls wanted to photograph a couple of ships when it dawned on my aging and decrepit brain that those decks would be awash with young sailors. "Sure," I said to the ladies, smiling. My suspicions were confirmed as they started to primp within a few seconds after I gave permission.

"Only one person out on that pulpit at a time," I ordered, looking at Annabelle but speaking loud enough for the others to hear.

The young men didn't mind going in close as they had never seen destroyers before and were interested in the kinds of armament they carried.

Soon, I got back on the mic of the CB.

Seawitch: *I'll be slowing down for a few minutes.*

Captain Indian: *OK, Seawitch. I'll go sit on the pile and hold them for you. Remember, we only got a six-hour trip."*

Captain Lobster: *Bob, why don't you ask them what they're doing?*

Seawitch: *Are you kidding?*

I knew full well that he wasn't.

Captain Lobster: *No, I'm not. Maybe they're looking for something and we can help them.*

Seawitch: *Sure, what the hell. I'll ask them.*

I made sure, through the binoculars, that the destroyers were indeed drifting and set my course for the first one, so as to approach her bow on slightly to his port. Captain Indian had changed course more to the north, as he didn't want anything to do with the ships and would pass them on his starboard side by at least 1,000 yards. When we were within 200 yards of the first one, I pulled back the power to trolling speed and changed my course so as to pass along the whole port side of this powerful sleep gray ship.

Somehow, I felt like a playful but cautious puppy approaching a Great Dane. There didn't appear to be any activity aboard the destroyer, but when I looked through binoculars, I could make out several men on the bridge eyeing us carefully, if not disdainfully.

I waved, then brought the Seawitch into a port turn and approached the port beam of the destroyer a little aft of her bridge section.

A sailor with a megaphone was scrambling down a bridge ladder, followed by another man whom I presumed was an officer. I was sure they were about to give us our marching orders when Annabelle and the girls climbed out on the bow and pulpit dressed in cutoffs, bikinis, and cameras. The affect was startling and from that moment on, I knew that I owned the destroyer.

"Good morning," said the obviously delighted sailor through the megaphone.

The girls waved and smiled, and the officers smiled back.

"What are you guys doing here?" I asked, looking up at the two men smiling at the girls as they leaned over the destroyer's railing.

The sailor looked at the officer.

"We had a little engine problem," the officer said. "So we came in here to fix it."

I nodded back and said something about it being a nice day to drift and do that sort of thing, all the while noticing that men were piling out of hatchways, scurrying up and down ladders, and fighting for a place along the rail. I waved goodbye and slowly trolled along the entire length of the ship while the girls put on a grand show, the camera clicking, their arms waving, and laughing at sailors who returned the sentiment with whistles, wolf calls, and numerous invitations for the ladies to come aboard. I was certain that the destroyer had taken on a five-degree list to port as we pulled away from her.

Our arrival at the second destroyer, which lay about 2,000 yards stern first to us and in a direct line to her sister ship, was a little bit different due, I think, to the advance billing probably sent along by the first ship's radio operator. We were greeted by camera-ready sailors who behaved pretty much the same way as the others had, and everyone had a lovely time of it.

"What are you fellows doing in the bay?" I shouted up to a group of officers as we trolled close along her starboard side.

"We got a small engine problem," one of the men said.

The Indian appeared to be a mile or so to the east from where we had previously fished the day before. However, I wouldn't alter course until he gave me the word.

I keyed the mic of the CB.

Seawitch: *You doing it?*

Captain Indian: *I'm tight now. Where are you?*

Seawitch: *We're about two miles from you. You on the pile?*

Captain Indian: *Yes, I got 'em. Come on over.*

I altered course about 15 degrees to starboard and pointed the pulpit at a white dot on a blue horizon.

Captain Lobster: *Seawitch, swing over.*

I reached for the CB channel selector and turned the dial.

Seawitch: *I'm here, Captain.*

Captain Indian: *Did you ask them what they're doing in here?*

Seawitch: *Yes, they told me they had engine problems.*

Captain Lobster didn't reply right away, and I assumed he was pulling a pot.

Captain Lobster: *Bullshit.*

Captain Lobster's voice was full of laughter.

Day 6

Mrs. Short rose at dawn, made her husband's breakfast, prepared his lunch box, and drove him to the harbor. She stopped at the post office, picked up the mail, then walked across the street to a card and gift shop, and spent an hour visiting her sister-in-law, who is the manager. After leaving, she did the marketing and starts home. She scarcely noticed a large tractor trailer truck that passed her on the main road as she was about to turn onto her street. However, she did notice that a black sedan with two men was parked beside the curb near its entrance. Mrs. Short drove up the street and turned into her driveway, exactly the same way she had done for over 35 years. She stepped from the vehicle, retrieved her market basket, and started for the kitchen door.

At this point, dear friends, Mrs. Short began to realize that something was wrong, but she couldn't quite come to grips with it. First, she looked from her house, then to the work shed, then back to the house. Mrs. Short then stopped walking and stared with a totally blank expression down her driveway. It took the poor woman a full minute to realize that the working shed was missing.

Day 7

Henry had not said a word to his wife during breakfast, simply because Mrs. Short had refused to speak to him and would continue to do so until he told her where the shed went and what all this nonsense was about.

"Henry," she said the following evening. "I have never interfered in your work, and I don't expect you to interfere in my house, but I will not be the laughing stock of this town. I mean, just what am I to say to people? That you sent a two-car garage and work shed out to be cleaned? How am I to explain it? What will the neighbors say?"

"The neighbors won't say anything," said Henry.

"Well then, just what am I to say if someone should ask?" demanded Mrs. Short.

"Tell them the termites got it or don't tell 'em nothing."

"Very well," Mrs. Short says her voice turning to ice. "I have nothing more to say to you."

Henry spent the night in the spare bedroom, dreading the future and ruing the day he pulled that damn thing out of the water. Why, the last time he slept in the spare bedroom it was six weeks before he got out, and that was because of some silly misunderstanding that occurred up in Boston at a seafood festival with Miss Lobster Queen of 1964. And now all this because of a damn can that went 'bleep'.

Day 8

Nothing spectacular happened this day. The destroyers left the bay and things seemingly slipped back into the usual busy summer routine.

Angel Base vectored one charter boat to an outboard that ran out of gas and another to a boy and girl on a 12-foot Sunfish that managed to get itself blown four miles off shore.

Captain Lobster did make one statement, however, that pointed out the fact that Henry hadn't used his radio for three days. He thought it was broken and Henry was too cheap to fix it. They continued the conversation on the radio.

Angel Base: *I agree. I think Lobster wants someone to pick on.*

Captain Lobster: *Crap. They're on to me again.*

Day 9

It was a Sunday morning, and Henry and Mrs. Short drove to church, as had been their custom most of their lives. Mrs. Short still hadn't spoken to her husband but did give him a sharp elbow to his ribs when their pastor begins a sermon on truth and honesty in our every day lives.

Henry sat there and took it, knowing full well that the pastor is Mrs. Short's first cousin. He was positive that this hour and a half thesis had been arranged for his benefit.

After service, they drove to Chatham and had dinner and spent the day with his relatives. Neither he nor Mrs. Short mentioned a thing about the events of the past week and both were grateful that their folks in Chatham know nothing of it. It was late afternoon when they pulled into their driveway.

"Oh my, Henry!" exclaimed Mrs. Short, breaking the silence.

Henry said nothing, but nodded approvingly at his new work shop and garage.

"I think you'll find everything to your liking, sir," said a tall, well-dressed man as he opened Mrs. Short's door.

"I bet it took 20 men to do that," said Henry.

"25, sir," answered the man.

"Well, let's have a look at her," said Henry.

"Allow me to show you around, Mrs. Short," offers the man taking her arm. "I think you'll enjoy this."

The new workshop had the same design as the old, but there was no resemblance after that. Row upon row of new hand tools took the place of old ones, and all the power tools had also been replaced. Mrs. Short found herself the owner of a new potting shed and greenhouse that had been attached to the back of the shop, also supplied with a complete set of tools.

"This must have cost a fortune," said Mrs. Short to her guide. "And how could you have done it so quickly?"

"As to your first question, Mrs. Short, all I can say is that it cost nothing compared to what it saved. And as to the second, well, we just had to get the Captain out of the dog house."

"Spare bedroom," said Mrs. Short.

"As you may," said the man, bowing slightly and smiling.

"I can't figure out why you boys wanted the building too," said Henry. "It ain't radioactive or something. I mean, us and the neighbors, are not going to get sick, are we?"

"No sir," the man said laughing. "That device was not anything like that. We took your building because of a foul up, and that's all I can say about it."

"Well can you tell me why that thing went 'bleep'?"

The tall man smiled at the Henry and his wife for a few seconds.

"I don't know what you're talking about," he said. "What thing?"

Chapter 11

Three Blind Mice

For those unaccustomed to fog on Cape Cod Bay, let me say it does not tip-toe in on little cat feet. No, no, dear reader. Let's think of it as something like several **Panzer** divisions bulldozing across the desert, for Khartoum. Then you'll be somewhere in the right ballpark. Our fog isn't a subtle gentle mist that nearly blocks the view. It's a thick, cold, gray mist that has the consistency of something less than number three bunker oil. Not only is it dangerous to navigate, it makes it almost impossible to fish, unless you have the right equipment, a lot of luck, and know well what you're doing.

The radio boat traffic as monitored on Channel 23 on the CB sounded like this. It began a little after 0530 hours on a late June morning in 1974.

Captain Lobster: *It's thick as shit, Magpie. I can't see my bow.*

Captain Magpie: *Well, I'm coming anyway, so you better get that slab outta the way!*

Captain Indian: *I hope your bubble machine (radar) is working cause I'm gonna keep my pulpit right on your ass.*

Captain Tramp: *Seawitch, you got three mosquitos (outboards, not charter boats) on your starboard going like hell.*

Seawitch: *You fellows in the outboards ought to stay inside till it burns off.*

Outboard No. 1: *Screw you.*

Outboard No. 2: *I'm going back in.*

Outboard No. 3: *Chicken shit.*

Orleans charter boat: *No better down this end. Black as hell.*

Captain Tramp: *Seawitch, you talk to P-town yet?*

Provincetown (P-town) charter boat: *You guys go home and play with the baby's momma.*

Captain Magpie: *Go play with yourself!*

P-town boat: *Now is that the way to say good morning to an old friend?*

Captain Magpie: *Damn right. You ought to stay home and count your money. How does it look up there?*

P-town boat: *Look! Look! Why you dizzy bastard. There ain't no look to it. You can't see 50 feet!*

Captain Tramp to Magpie: *I bet he's lying and probably sitting on the pile (over a school of fish).*

Captain Magpie: *You say he's got piles?*

Captain Lobster: *Oh, sweet mystery of life. At last I've found you. Da da dee, da da doo.*

Captain Indian: *What the hell was that?*

Seawitch: *Captain Lobster singing.*

Captain Indian: *Oh, I thought my set was dying. Oooh Oooh.*

Seawitch: *What happened?*

Captain Indian: *This guy in an outboard almost ran into me. Tried to cut between Magpie and me. I almost got his outrigger.*

Seawitch: *Captain Lobster, where are you working?*

Captain Lobster: *30 degrees* **second string**.

Captain Magpie: *Now I can cut him in half.*

Captain Lobster (in a weak voice): *Motherrrrr ...*

Outboard No. 2: *Johnny, can you and Bobby come back here?*

Outboard No. 3: *Come back where? What way is back?*

Outboard No. 2: *210 degrees. I just broke a control cable. I got no throttle.*

Outboard No. 2's wife (from shore radio): *You got no brains either for going out there. I told you not to go, dim wit.*

Seawitch: *You guys better throw the hook and wait till it burns off.*

Captain Magpie: *I got you outboards on radar. You're three-quarters of a mile from the bell. Go back 240 degrees. Your friend is a half mile from the bell.*

Outboard No. 2: *I'm in 40 feet of water and drifting.*

Captain Tramp: *You better throw the hook. You got an outgoing tide.*

Seawitch: *That's what I told him.*

Outboard No. 2: *I got lobster pots around me. Black ones.*

Captain Lobster: *What's the number on the pots?*

Outboard No. 2: *17 and maybe 21, I think. It's hard to see, but it's 20 something.*

Captain Lobster: *You drop your anchor and when I go in I'll pick you up, I know where you are.*

Outboard No. 2: *When you going in?*

Captain Lobster: *When I'm done pulling pots, Sonny. You stay there. Three or four hours at most.*

Outboard No. 2: *Thanks, Captain. We'll wait.*

Outboard No. 3: *Don't worry Tommy. We're coming. You won't have to wait.*

Outboard No. 1: *Yeah Tommy, we'll be there in ...*

A moment of silence went by before Outboard No. 2 tried to reach his friends, but they didn't answer. The Captain Lobster called Outboard No. 2 and made certain that they had an anchor out. Outboard No. 2 confirmed this and kept trying to reach his friends. It wasn't until several more minutes had passed before he got a reply.

Outboard No. 1 to Outboard No. 2: *We hear you, dummy. Just wait a minute.*

Outboard No. 2: *What happened? How come you guys don't answer?*

Outboard No. 3: *We both missed the bell and ran aground. I almost ripped the motor off my transom. Sons of a bitch! My rig's all screwed up.*

Outboard No. 2: *How's Bobby?*

Outboard No. 3: *Cripes, he hit so hard he went halfway through his windshield! He's all cut up and his rig is full of water. He knocked a hole in it when he hit.*

Outboard No. 2: *Where are you?*

Outboard No. 3 started to answer, but Outboard No. 1 broke in shouting into the mic.

Outboard No. 1: *How in the hell do we know? We're on a sand bar somewhere!*

Captain Tramp to Outboards: *It's a damn wonder you guys are not dead, running full-speed in this crap. Stand by. We'll try to get some help to you.*

Captain Lobster to Captain Tramp: *I'll call Angel. Maybe they can get some help down the beach. It wouldn't be bad if those bastards only killed themselves, but they make it dangerous for everyone running around like that.*

Angel Base to fleet: *I've been listening fellows. I called the rescue squad and they'll take care of it. I'll be standing by.*

Outboard No. 2 to Captain Lobster: *Hey Captain. We got our throttle fixed. Just a loose nut. Thanks.*

Captain Lobster: *Three blind mice. Three blind mice. See how they run. See how they run ...*

Chapter 12

Overdue

The early June sun had wrung the dampness out of the morning air as we knifed our way through a flat sea toward the southern edge of **Billingsgate Shoal.** We were one of five Barnstable charter boats, spaced approximately at 2,000-yard intervals. So far, our search for the season's first good run of striped bass had been fruitless. Several boats had called out to charter and private vessels from other harbors for information, but other than a few small fish taken near Wellfleet by one of the Provincetown boys, no one had anything good to report. My mate, Bobby — a young police officer who worked the night shift and daylighted as a fisherman to earn extra money as he was an expectant father — appeared to be apprehensive and more nervous than usual.

"What's wrong, kid?" I asked, smiling. "You worried?"

"Yeah. These damn fish are overdue and so is Linda."

"Well if I turned this boat around and brought you in, would you feel better?"

"Yeah, but if there was no reason, Linda would have my head. She made me promise."

"Promise what?" I asked.

"She made me promise not to hang around the house after work. Says I drive her crazy."

"Do you?"

"Yeah, I guess so. But she's supposed to take it easy and do what the doc says, but a lot of times she doesn't."

"Well maybe it's just as well you're out here. This way you can give her some peace and earn a little money while you're doing it.

"I know. You, her, and the doc say the same thing, but I can't help what I feel," sighed Bobby.

Soon our radio came to life with a call.

Angel Base: *Seawitch.*

Seawitch: *Go ahead, Angel.*

Angel Base: *Switch over.*

I turned the channel selector to a side band setting and Angel was waiting as I keyed the mic.

Seawitch: *What's up, sweetheart?*

Angel Base: *Seawitch. There's a call for you on Channel 11. I'll go get him; you stand by.*

Seawitch: *This wouldn't be for my mate, would it?*

Angel Base: *No, it's from the Upchuck, a private boat.*

I watched the color return to Bobby's face, as I waited for the 'Upchuck' to come on the channel.

"Go aft and make sure everything's set. This may be what we're looking for," I instructed him.

"Everything is set, I just checked," he said.

"Well, go back and tell the people what to expect if we hit fish, and cut the worrying. If anything happens, I'll have you back at the dock in 30 minutes."

The radio came to life again.

> Captain Upchuck: *Seawitch, are you ground fishing today or looking for the big stuff?*

> Seawitch: *Big stuff — striped bass.*

> Captain Upchuck: *Well, we're mackerel fishing! And we just had a rod busted. This the—*

The radio went dead for a second then came back garbled as two men were trying to talk at the same time.

> Seawitch: *Slow down fellows. I can't understand. You'll have to speak clearly and one at a time.*

> Captain Upchuck: *I was bringing in a mackerel and this silver fish about five feet long came up and took it and busted my rod all to hell! Couldn't hold him.*

> Seawitch: *OK.*

I was looking around at the boats on both sides. I knew that the minute Angel called, that they switched channels along with us and were listening.

> Seawitch: *You want to give us a location, Upchuck? We all would appreciate it.*

Captain Upchuck: *Seawitch, we're about one mile west of the Barn-stable Bell and we're in 40 feet of water.*

Seawitch: *Thank you, Upchuck.*

I threw the boat out of gear and gave Bobby the hall-in-the-lines sign.

Captain Upchuck: *Seawitch, how big do bass get?*

Seawitch: *Well Upchuck, five feet is a good one and some even get bigger.*

The air went still except for a few mumbled words.

Captain Upchuck: *Seawitch, could we borrow a rod if you come here? We'll bring it back to you in the harbor.*

Seawitch: *Sure thing, no problem. We'll be there soon.*

Bobby lifted the last rig over the stern as I added power, throwing rainbows in our wake between us and the morning sun.

"What is it now?" I shouted, looking back at the mate as he came forward shrugging his shoulders and looking for all the world like the astonished little kid who had just discovered there was no Santa Claus.

"They don't want to fish," he answered wringing his hands at me. "They came out here, and they don't want to fish."

I motioned frustrated Bobby to the wheel and went aft to join the two young couples, who from their smiles and laughter were obviously enjoying themselves.

"I didn't have much time to chat when you folks came aboard," I said to the foursome. "I hope you're having a good time."

A small, dark-haired girl with a ponytail, named Jenny, grinned showing twin rows of white teeth. "Oh man! Like, wow! Like, this is a scream!" she said beaming at me, then turning toward her young man, Joe. "Ain't this, like, a scene?" His eyes caught hers, then focused to the four boats steaming with us in a line abreast.

"Oh! Like, you know it," Joe said watching the boats push through the gold-green sea. "Like, you know it, like, it is a scene."

The other twosome nodded agreement with their friends. "Out of sight. Just out of sight," they chimed.

"Well, why doesn't anyone want to fish?" I asked.

"Oh, like killing is not our bag and we don't eat meat," Jenny stated as Joe nestled her in his arms.

"We came just to go out on the sea and ride around. Isn't that OK?"

"Sure it is," I nodded. "But that doesn't mean you can't enjoy fishing."

"But we don't want to kill anything," the other young man, Jim, said.

"You don't have to," I explained. "We catch fish, take their weight and measurements, even their pictures, and release them unharmed. We do it all the time."

"That may be cool, but for me, I'll just watch," said Joe.

"Yeah. Like, we'll just watch and be cool, if that's OK," said Jim.

"Like, out of sight. Out of sight. That's cool," I said laughing.

Jenny giggled. "Oh wow! He understands. He understands."

I made my way back to the helm and took the mic from my mate.

"What the hell is so funny?" my puzzled mate asked as I took his place.

"Nothing at all," I said. "I was just enjoying the articulate and definitive English the young folks were using to describe this voyage and the surroundings."

"Are they going to fish?" Bobby asked.

"No, my dear constable. You are, and will be releasing."

The puzzled look instantly changed to an unbelieving one that slowly gave way to the most relaxed and pleasant expression I had seen on his face that day.

"Out of sight. I can dig it," he said.

A clear voice came alive over the VHF.

Captain Magpie: *Seawitch?*

I didn't bother to answer the set but picked up my binoculars and focused them on the flying bridge of the 'Magpie', which was the closest boat on our starboard side. The skipper was waving his binoculars and pointing at the horizon directly forward. I waved back and turned my attention to what the naked eye would perceive to be an empty expanse of sea. Through the glasses, I could make out tiny white specks that were seagulls lazily crisscrossing an expanse of water about two miles ahead of us. Beyond them, a small green boat outlined itself against the shore.

Seawitch: *Upchuck, are you still on the channel?*

Captain Upchuck: *This is Upchuck. Over. Who's calling?*

Seawitch: *This is the Seawitch, Upchuck. What color is your hull? Come back.*

Captain Upchuck: *We're green, Seawitch. Over.*

Seawitch: *Anything else happen, gentlemen?*

Captain Upchuck: *We don't have the right stuff Seawitch, but every now and then, these bass come up splash around, and there are millions of birds around us.*

I let go of the mic and went back to the binoculars.

Captain Magpie: *Look off his stern!*

Bobby ducked under me and took the wheel as I studied the glasses with both hands. At first, there was just the green boat and more gulls overhead, but as I focused to his stern, I could make out a few funneling flickering specks of white.

Bobby caught my attention and pointed to the Magpie as it, and a boat to our portside, poured on the coal and left ahead of the line.

Seawitch: *Go ahead. Let's get down there. They may not stay up for long.*

I went back to the glasses, as the sound of the diesel changed from a deep throttled hum to a high-volume roar.

Captain Upchuck: *Tally ho!*

Then another voice on the same set said something about sounding the charge.

The scene through the glasses changed considerably as we closed the distance. The sky and sea for a square mile aft of the green boat was filled with hundreds of funneling, diving **turns** along with flocks of dark shearwaters crisscrossing a foot or so about the surface. Seagulls by the score rafted on the sea, while at least a thousand other swooped lazily through and above the other birds.

Seawitch: *Upchuck, how long has this been going on?*

Captain Upchuck: *Is that you, Seawitch?*

Seawitch: *Yes, Upchuck. How long has the birds been here?*

Captain Upchuck: *About an hour, Seawitch. They stated coming right after them fish started splashing around and we lost ... Seawitch, I can see a bunch of boats steaming this way. Are you one of them?*

Seawitch: *That's right, fellows. Are the fish still breaking?*

Captain Upchuck: *Yes, Seawitch, but not as much as before.*

Seawitch: *Thanks, Upchuck. I'll pass a rod to you as soon as we get settled.*

At a quarter mile from the birds we started reducing power along with the rest of our fleet and began setting out lines.

Bobby measured out two wire lines to distance so that they ran about 15 feet below the surface, and I lowered the starboard outrigger, so a single lure should be trolled just on the surface and far back of the two wires. As the engine slowed, the screeching, screaming, and chattering of the birds filled the air along with shouts of "oh wow" and "out of sight" by my young customers.

Again the radio came alive.

Captain Upchuck: *Seawitch, when you get a minute.*

I finished thumbing out the starboard lines and grabbed the mic.

Seawitch: *Go ahead, Captain.*

Captain Upchuck: *Why don't you and Magpie come this way?*

I turned to port and lined the bow up on a large white boat that was stopped.

Captain Upchuck: *Two lines tight.*

Captain Magpie: *Up or down?*

Captain Upchuck: *Both ways; and one's got my outrigger stripped.*

"Like, what they are saying?" asked Joe. "What's tight?"

Bobby explained that the white boat had just hooked two fish and was fighting them, and one of the fish had taken a surface lure that had been attached to the outrigger and stripped off all the line on the reel, while the other fish had hit a deep-trolled lure on wire.

"Oh, like, man, that's cool," he said to Bobby. "But you guys ought to learn to speak English, so people could understand."

My mate's face took on a pink glow beneath his suntan while the beginning of a word formed on his lips like a bubble of fresh lava beneath the thin crust of a volcano. However, I stopped the eruption by flopping him over the head with my baseball cap and calling him a square and demanding that he go back to college and learn cool.

Captain Magpie: *Marking at 20 feet.*

I checked out our fathometer and flipped on the record switch.

Captain Upchuck: *It was a 30 pounder; and we dropped the other one!*

Several hundred turns wheeled and began funneling less than 50 feet off our port bow. Then suddenly thousands of small sand eels showered on the surface followed by a tremendous explosion of white water as several silver and lime colored fish arched themselves free of the sea.

"Marking," said Bobby. "The whole damn school is right under..."

The unfinished words seemed to hang in the air as the whirl of a high-speed ratchet blurred out all other sound.

Seawitch: *Tight on a wire.*

I threw the engine out of gear.

My four young customers froze as the sight and sound of the violently whipping rod. I doffed my hat and made a sweeping bow to the young policeman.

"You may fish when ready, Bobby," I said.

Jenny's friend, Julie, had been next to the rod as the fish struck and she regained her voice, all she could manage was an, "Oh golly."

Bobby was about five seconds into the first fish when the second rod started grinding. I was about to pop the outrigger line free when a third fish saved us the trouble.

"Oh darn!" Julie screamed as her fish took a deep powerful lunge. "Oh wow!"

The CB began to crackle.

Angel Base: *Seawitch?*

Captain Magpie: *Angel, he's into a triple.*

He watched us turn into the school of breaking fish.

Captain Magpie: *Give him a minute to get settled.*

Angel Base: *Thanks, Captain. And Seawitch, you switch over when you're ready.*

I set a light drag on the outrigger line and passed it to Julie. "Just hang on, honey," I ordered. "I'll be right back."

I hit the channel selector and keyed the mic.

Seawitch: *Go ahead, Angel.*

Angel Base: *I just got that phone call you've been expecting.*

I immediately turned down the volume and checked aft to see if Bobby had heard.

Jenny had reached the point in her battle when she was wondering just who had hooked whom. And from her screaming and cursing, she loved every second of it.

"I never thought I'd do this. I never ... oh wow! Ooooh wow!"

Bobby had adjusted the drag on the second fish and was too busy supervising Jenny and fighting his own striper to have heard a thing.

Seawitch: *OK, Angel. What's the word?*

Angel Base: *Well, Seawitch, she just went into labor and his sergeant is sending a cruiser for her. They'll be at the hospital in 30 minutes.*

I said thanks and flipped the set back to our working channel and called the Upchuck.

Upchuck: *Do what?!*

Seawitch: *Just work up to my starboard. We're going to pass a rod with a fish on it to you."*

Magpie came back on the air and began giving Angel a play-by-play description of the activities on my boat when two of his rods bent over and turned his cockpit into a Chinese fire drill.

Bobby managed to work his fish alongside: a beautiful lime and silver 25-pounder. After a few seconds of "oh wows" and "out of sights," I reached over with a pair of pliers and snapped the fish free.

Jenny, on the other hand, stopped screaming, but continued cursing under her breath until her fish, a twin to Bobby's, bellied up a few feet off the stern.

"You're wonderful!" she said looking at her fish and catching her breath. "You're just wonderful."

Joe snapped a picture or two while I set the fish free.

Then everyone scrambled to the starboard as the small green outboard swung in close to pick up the outrigger rod.

"Time to go," I announced to them all. "We got to get in."

"Hey man! Like, this is fun, and ain't we got the boat till 1 o'clock?" questioned Joe.

"That's right," I said. "But Bobby's wife is on the way to the hospital to have their first child, and I think we'd better get him in fast."

Jenny and Julie screamed and jumped up and down. "A baby!" they squealed. "A new little baby!"

Bobby's lower jaw took a dive for the deck while I poured on the power and sped away from the fleet.

A shiny, new cruiser with lights flashing was waiting with its door open as we slipped into the dock.

"We'd like to come too," begged the girls as all of us ran up the ramp to see Bobby off.

"Hey, OK," he said grinning. "Let's all go."

The ride into Hyannis was just as spectacular as the quick trip in on the Seawitch. We arrived just 25 minutes ahead of Bobby's lovely young daughter. When all the cheering, hugging, and kissing has quieted down in the waiting room, his face took on a thoughtful expression.

"You know, Captain, this morning everything was overdue."

I nodded my head. "You're right," I agreed.

"Like, out of sight," he said breaking into laughter.

"Out of sight."

Chapter 13

Mrs. Palmer Gasnold and Her After-Action Report (or The Road to Hell is Paved with Good Intentions)

The only introduction I feel that's suitable for the following short narrative that occurred on a summer's morning a long time ago is a short one.

I was skippering a sport-fishing yacht that belonged to a Vice President of General Hydraulics, who had invited several of his young, up-and-coming executives and their wives aboard for a day's outing. We had pulled into the fuel dock to fill our tanks, which were down to less than one-quarter of their capacity, when I was approached by one of the guests who told me that he would take care of the fuel. I thought nothing of it and pointed to the yard boy who was running the high-speed pump.

"Take care of it with him," I said. "He'll tell you how much it is when he's done."

The young man went for a short stroll, then returned to the pump just as the yard boy was writing out the slip.

"Check or credit card?" asked the man.

"Do you take cash?" asked the man.

"Sure," said the kid looking a little surprised. "If you like."

"How much is it?" the man asked smiling and reaching for his wallet at the same time.

"$845.30," said the kid.

"What?" said the junior executive leaning closer to the kid and turning a little green.

"800 and 45 dollars and 30 cents, sir. You took on over 1,000 gallons."

It was at this point that I stepped off the boat and came to man's rescue. "Look," I said. "Why don't you let them put it on the boat's yard bill. You wouldn't want to mess up your boss's bookkeeping, would you?"

"Certainly not!" exclaimed the rising junior executive as color returned to his face. "Thank you."

This incident had a happy ending because I was able to make a difference and save a man from his good intentions.

However, try as I may, there was no listening to me or anyone else the day Palmer Gasnold caught his first, and probably last, tuna fish.

What a picture-perfect day it had been. Our morning was spent blue fishing and shortly before noon, Annabelle, my mate, announced that everyone was ready for a try at tuna. A small five-pound blue was rigged with two single hooks, which did its job tying us fast to a good fish that we boated in a little less than two hours.

Palmer Gasnold had done an excellent job in the fighting chair and was pleased as punch when his fish tipped the scales at 647 pounds. Palmer had booked the trip for blues only and had taken 25 fish, which was what it took to fill his two coolers with fillets. Palmer asked us if he could give tuna a try and what would the extra cost be.

I told him there would be no extra cost involved, but we would keep the fish and sell it.

Palmer happily agreed to this but had a change of heart shortly after the picture-taking ceremony was over.

Mrs. Gasnold was flabbergasted at her husband's statement. "You're going to what?" she asked.

"I'm going to keep the fish. I caught it, and I am going to keep it. For goodness sakes, Betina. We'll share it with our friends. And I intend to put some away in the freezer."

Mrs. Gasnold looked to the sky, then turned to me. "Please, Captain," she begged. "Talk some sense into my husband. He's out of his mind."

I took Palmer aside and explained that the fish was worth a dollar a pound to us and we agreed to take him tuna fishing on the condition that we keep the fish. And we had not charged him for a tuna trip.

"I agree, Captain, and I intend to pay you for the tuna, as well as the trip. You're an honorable man and so am I."

"I think you're making a mistake," I explained. "Please listen to your wife. That's a hell of a lot of fish there."

"Captain, I have made up my mind. If you and your mate will load the fish in the back of my car, I'll make out your check."

Annabelle backed Palmer's new Cadillac Eldorado up to the Hoist and, with the help of several bystanders and the use of a small ladder as a ramp, we slid the tuna head first into the car's trunk and tied down the lid. Palmer gave us a check for the trip, which included the following amounts:

- One blue fishing trip: $225

- One tuna fish: $647

- Tip for the captain and mate: $25 each.

The total amount of the check was $922. Palmer thanked us profusely, ignored our pleas, and departed in his stern-down Cadillac, which looked like a giant wind-up toy because of the large crescent shaped tail that protruded from its rear.

That was the last I was to see of Palmer Gasnold and, had it not been for a letter from Mrs. Gasnold the following week canceling a late September bass trip and a long telephone conversation with the dear woman, I wouldn't have gotten the rest of the story.

Mrs. Gasnold explained in detail the following events, which began the moment they left Barnstable and ended five days later.

"Thank goodness," Mrs. Gasnold said. "Had it not been for the police and the sympathy of her close friends, Palmer would have been tarred and feathered and displayed in a cage in downtown Darion, Connecticut."

In order to fully appreciate the following events, I have written the rest of this narrative in the form of an expense diary with explanations, beginning on August 25th, the morning of the fishing trip, and ending August 30th, after Mrs. Gasnold's court appearance.

August 25th

- Auto fuel: $21.65

- Breakfast for four: $12.60

- Fishing trip: $922

- Dinner for four: $58

- Drinks with friends at country club in Darion that evening: $41.30

- Estimated cost of replacing two rear leaf springs in Cadillac: $426.80

August 26th

In order to unload the tuna fish from his Cadillac, Mr. Gasnold backed his vehicle into the garage, which was built sometime in the mid-1920s. This building was made of fieldstone and had a wood frame slate roof. Mr. Gasnold, with the help of a neighbor, tied one end of a sturdy rope around the tail of the tuna and the other end over the top of the center crossbeam of the building. The idea was to pull ahead slowly, letting the rope pull the tuna out of the trunk of the car.

That wasn't a bad idea, except that when Mr. Gasnold eased the car ahead under her neighbor's direction, the gill cover of the fish slipped over the trunk latch and held firm. Mr. Gasnold eased back a little and the gill cover unhooked. When his neighbor inspected the fish, he could find no obstruction and instructed Mr. Gasnold to pull ahead a little faster this time. Well friends, what happened at this point was an exercise in elementary physics. The car shot forward, the fish's gill cover hooked the trunk's latch, which ripped back the trunk wall. The fish pulled free, then swung backward striking the rear stone wall of the garage, collapsing it. The slate roof started to buckle and then fell as the right wall of the garage crumbled outward in a cloud of dust and debris. When the dust settled, half a wall was left standing and collapsed slate roof weighing tons was lying on top of Palmer Gasnold's tuna.

- Estimated cost of body work on auto trunk: $316.21

- Hospital and emergency room cost for neighbor: $290.30

- Estimated cost of garage replacement: $7,941.50

August 27th

Palmer Gasnold left for work on time, and Mrs. Gasnold spent most of the morning making arrangements with a contractor to remove the remains of the garage. The contractor, a burly man by the name of Costolani, informed Mrs. Gasnold that the earliest his men could begin work was on August 31st.

Late in the afternoon, the temperature in Darion reached 92 degrees, making it the third day in a row to do so. This is also the second day that Palmer's Tuna had laid under the fallen black slate roof.

• Estimated cost of rubble and debris removal: $1,175

August 28th

Mr. Gasnold, upon the urging of Mrs. Gasnold, took the day off, and late in the morning he and Mrs. Gasnold inspected the sight of their late garage. They were met by 842,758,921 flies and other insects that had taken up residence with the tuna under the slate roof. The aroma emanating from the sight took less than 30 seconds to make a distinct impression upon the Gasnolds, and they fled the scene in record time.

Mr. Gasnold spent an hour on the telephone tracking down Mr. Costolani, who eventually agreed to send workmen with the appropriate tools to hack through the fallen roof and a dump truck to cart the carcass away. Mr. Costolani informed Mr. Gasnold that this would cost extra and that a boat will have to be hired to tow the carcass out to sea, as it will not be accepted at the town dump. Mr. Gasnold happily agreed to this and Mr. Costolani assured Mr. Gasnold that his men would start work the following morning. Mr. Gasnold begged Mr. Costolani to come sooner, but the contractor said that is impossible.

As the temperature rose, a gentle southwest wind flowed evenly over the quiet little town of Darion, and by 2 o'clock the Gasnolds received no fewer than a dozen phone calls from neighbors expressing their opinions, especially those who live down wind of the Gasnolds. As a matter of record, all outdoor activities within a quarter mile of the Gasnold residence has come to an abrupt halt.

By late afternoon the Gasnolds had received three delegations: the first from the Board of Health; the second a committee of formerly friendly neighbors; and the third from the police department with a summons issued by a district court judge, who just happened to reside a few houses away from the Gasnold property. Cost estimate:

- Removal of tuna fish: $270

- Transportation to New Haven: $130

- Towing charge of charter boat: $200

- Replacement of front window, which was broken by a note-carrying rock: $175

August 29th

Mr. Costolani arrived with two workmen shortly before 9 a.m. and both men refused to work without gas masks. However, these items were borrowed from the local fire department, and by noon, to the relief of everyone, the remains of Palmer Gasnold's tuna fish were trucked away, followed by most of the 842,758,000 and some odd flies.

Mr. Gasnold arrived at court at the appointed time with his attorney, Mr. Wineburg, who advised Mr. Gasnold to plead guilty and fall on the mercy of the court. Mr. Gasnold took his attorney's advice and was given a tongue-lashing, along with a $300 fine, the largest amount allowed by law.

Meanwhile, Mrs. Gasnold packed her bags and left to live in Westport with their daughter, claiming that she is socially ruined in Darion society and can never show her face in the community again.

- Expenditures to date: $12,280.36

September 4th

Mrs. Gasnold returned home after several days of negotiations with Mr. Gasnold and on the condition that he never fished again. Expenses:

- Flowers: $67

- New fall wardrobe for Mrs. Gasnold: $1,150

- Total Expenses: $13,497.96 (not even including lawyer and court charges)

Chapter 14

Jones

On all the logbooks that cover my 40 years at sea, one stands out as a beacon, or a sore thumb as the facts may prove. It was the year that we suffered more calamities and accidents than any other.

The reason for this was a single person, a young woman who came and worked as my mate. It was not her fault that these occurred, but it was her looks that incited them. I felt that it was somewhat of a great cosmic joke.

I feel that somewhere in paradise in the baby design department, a group of angels took some time off and decided to combine their celestial talents and create, with the good Lord's blessing, the most beautiful child that they could think of.

The late Al Capp, creator of the comic strip, Li'l Abner, came up with a character he called Stupefyin' Jones. Any man who looked at her would go gaga and temporarily out of their minds. And in truth, this young lady was a Stupefyin' Jones.

In the first month of her employment, we had two young men misstep our dock and fall into the water; three cases of fish hooks in fingers and hands, one of which required a trip to the hospital; and Lord know how many bumped and bruised heads.

The only response that I ever received from Jones was perhaps they were not paying attention. Well, dear reader, they were paying attention as they were totally absorbed in Stupifyin' Jones.

Now, this young woman didn't think of herself as anything special, "I'm just an average person," she said.

Jones, as far as I could tell, did not have a romantic thought in her mind. She did not date and had no significant other. Jones had a passion all right and somehow. When the angels designed her, they gave her a brain right out of Popular Mechanics. This young woman could and would take apart and repair anything.

The first time she came aboard the Seawitch, I had the hatch covers open for an oil and fluid change. "Oh my," she squealed in delight. "A Perkins Rolls Royce diesel, is it the 510M?"

"Yes," I answered.

"And that must be a Borg Warner 2½ to one gear," she added.

"Why yes," I mumbled.

"Can I help?" she said not taking her eyes off the big engine.

"Sure," I managed to blurt out. "But you are going to get dirty."

She wasn't paying attention to my words, as she was enraptured by the sight of the big diesel.

Within a month, this young woman mastered every mechanical and electrical object on the Seawitch. She detailed, stripped down, and repaired and cleaned every reel on the boat, along with any and everything related to the boat, including my ancient diesel pickup truck.

By mid-summer she had mastered all the knots required on a charter vessel, as well as inventing a few of her own, all of which were very useful and extraordinary in how they worked.

I remember a party of engineers from Sikorsky Aircraft who were huddled in the stern discussing a problem with a new design that was causing too much vibration. Jones, who was nearby, overheard this and stepped into the midst of this group.

"I know how to fix it," she said. "All you have to do is drill holes in it; that will stop the vibrating."

The men smiled politely at the lovely face and nodded their heads with a somewhat condescending attitude. However, within the week, a large company car from Sikorsky pulled up to our dock and two men presented a letter of thanks and a large check to Jones, along with a promise of a job interview when she finished school.

"How did you know to do this?" they asked.

Jones smiled her smile. "Toilet paper," she answered. "It seldom tears along the perforation."

It was during her second season aboard the Seawitch when her guardian angels agreed that romance should be introduced into her life. This came in the form of a young man, a one Larry Wenkowsky or Lug Wrench, as he was called by his family and friends. Lug was about one inch taller than Jones and was built with powerful arms and shoulders. He was a rather plain looking fellow and wore glasses. However, if there was ever a gyro gear loose, it was this young man. As an honor student at MIT, Lug had excelled. His mind worked like a computerized clock. Nevertheless, to put it mildly, when the two of them met, it was like they got stuck in second gear or struck by lightning. Lug showed up one hour early for a day of tuna fishing with his dad and uncle. Jones was oiling a 140T Penn Reel while sitting on the engine box in her summer uniform, a yellow bikini covered by a white t-shirt. I don't believe she had worn shoes since late May.

"What's the gear speed?" he asked, looking down at her. She turned, and their eyes met.

"2 ½ to 1," she managed to say after a long moment. "But I believe it's a bit faster."

"Yes, I think so," he whispered, not taking his eyes off her.

"The line speed increases with each turn of the... "

At this point words between them were useless, while they just stared at each other for a long moment.

"Want to see the diesel?" she eventually managed to ask.

He just nodded, not taking his eyes off her.

By the end of the day, their party had boated a 515-pound tuna and Jones had landed a 195-pound engineer.

Chapter 15

A Blitz of a Wedding

The wedding of Lug and Stupifyin' Jones came about a little over a year and seven months after their first meeting. However, several of their friends and relatives thought it should have occurred sooner, as they had become inseparable.

The wedding was to take place in mid-June. Lug and Jones decided it should be aboard the Seawitch. The party would consist of the bride, the groom, the best man, the maid of honor, a minister, and myself. The reception would be held at the Barnstable Marina in the large hanger, and there would be a little fewer than 150 attending.

The care and planning for these nuptials went forward beginning in late winter and throughout the spring. All the details had been carefully worked out and any change in the weather was factored in. However, nature had a bag of tricks and an agenda all her own.

At certain times during the season, game fish take a vacation; that is, they stop feeding. It isn't that they vacate the area, it is that they don't eat.

Once or twice during the summer this occurs. It may last for a few days or several weeks, and at the time of the wedding, there had been little or no activity for a little less than three weeks.

Charter boats all along the Cape sat idle. Restaurants and fish markets went begging for fresh fish, and the price paid by wholesalers went through the roof.

During this span of time, we kept busy doing maintenance, rebuilding, and repairing equipment and taking out a few sightseeing and sunset cruises.

The Saturday morning of the wedding was post card perfect, not a cloud in sight. The sea was deep blue and there wasn't a ripple on the surface.

The wedding party arrived at 10 a.m., along with several carloads of friends to see them off. The plan was to sail out to the harbor entrance bell (about three miles), perform the ceremony, and return to the dock and reception.

The party showed up on time, looking like a committee from the Good Humor Ice Cream Company: everyone was in white. Miss Jones wore a simple white dress with a pale blue ribbon braided into her hair, which fell over her left shoulder. She wore white nail polish and her only jewelry was her engagement ring from Lug and a silver ankle bracelet that her father had given her on her 16th birthday.

Lug wore white slacks, white leather loafers, a pale blue shirt with a white tie and sports jacket. Her maid of honor had a lovely white pantsuit, while the best man and minister wore white Bermuda shorts, white socks, and white shoes.

It was only a few minutes after the vows were taken, and I was about to start the diesel to head in, as we had been drifting to seaward on an outgoing tide, when our radio came to life.

Captain Lobster: *Seawitch, is that you a little north of the bell?*

Seawitch: *Sure is.*

Captain Lobster: *Swing over.*

I turned on our FM radio to our private channel.

Seawitch: *What's up?*

Captain Lobster: *Take a careful look to the northeast and tell me what you see.*

The new Mrs. Lug handed me my binoculars, and in less than 15 seconds I gave them back to her and got on the radio.

Captain Lobster: *What did you see?*

Seawitch: *Birds, thousands of them.*

Gulls, turns and shearwaters and mother Corey's chickens filled the sky about 2 ½ miles from us.

Captain Lobster: *Squid. I saw them on the surface in front of me 10 minutes ago.*

At this point, I must explain the significance of this sighting. Nothing in God's ocean is more appetizing to striped bass than squid. It is their most sought after and favorite food. They throw caution to the wind and themselves on the squid. They will feed 'till they can't hold anymore, yet they still go on killing.

I was about to ask the new Mrs. Lug if she remembered the wholesale price of stripers. However, she had read my thought and looked me straight in the face. "$2.50 a pound as of yesterday," she said.

For the next few moments, the Seawitch appeared to be a game of musical chairs. Rods and equipment were brought on deck, along with boxes of red, blue, and brown hoochers, a type of bait that looks like a squid. Gaff hooks and plyers were laid out on the gunnel. Three OT Soby hooks were checked for a 30-degree offset and their barbs bent flat, as we had learned that a 30-degree offset hook was seldom thrown and the other benefit was the fish could be unhooked instantly on deck.

"You're all wearing white," I said to this crew.

"Oh my god," screamed the new Mrs. Lug. "I can't fish in this dress."

Within a few minutes, she and the rest of the crew were in their underwear with bath towels wrapped around their waists and in their bare feet.

We were less than 1,000 yards from the main body of birds when the surface directly in front of our bow erupted as hundreds of large silver fish tore into a school of reddish-brown squid.

Five rods were set out, two flat outriggers lines trailed red hoochers on the surface at 125 feet. Three wire lines were set at 150 feet on port, starboard, and amid ship. Strike drags were set loose and clickers turned on.

I knew that these fish would hit with such force that no drag would be needed to set a hook. It was less than a minute after fifth rod was in its holder that the screen on our sonar went white. "Get set, here they come," I said to the crew.

The newly married Mrs. Lug was holding on to the handle of the starboard outrigger when 25 pounds of silver dynamite tore it loose from the pin. "Fish on," she screamed as her rod arched over. Within a few seconds, the remaining four rods were bent over with fighting on.

I keyed the mic on my radio.

Seawitch: *Lobster, we're very busy. I'm leaving my CB off.*

Captain Lobster: *Gotch' you.*

Within an hour and 15 minutes, our fish box was full, and the deck was littered with several hundred pounds of stripers. We had turned a lovely clean boat into a slaughterhouse. Needless to say, our wedding party looked like the blood-splattered victims and fiends from a third-rate horror movie.

We were over an hour and a half late getting back to the dock, and there were over 50 wedding guests waiting for us and wondering what the hell had happened.

When the Seawitch pulled into the dock, they could not believe their eyes: everyone but the captain was covered in blood-splattered underwear. The bride and her maid of honor had tied beach towels around their bottoms. Nevertheless, within an hour, the fish had been off loaded and trucked off and weighed in at a little over 1,000 pounds.

The bride and her maid of honor showed up at the reception wearing clean, dry dungarees, bare foot, and their damp hair wrapped in towels.

It turned out to be a wonderful celebration. Miss Jones was now Mrs. Lug, the fishing dry spell had ended, and we had made money.

"How much did we make?" Mrs. Lug asked.

"Well over $2,000," I said. "And I didn't make a thing; it's all yours, as my wedding gift to you."

"Oh my God," she whispered as her eyes filled with tears.

"No, Mrs. Lug," I told her. "I'm just your captain."

Two years later, the Wenkowsky's brought a son into the world, an 8-pound boy, and he was given my middle name of Randolph. Randolph Lawrence Wenkowsky, and Tinker was his nickname.

Chapter 16

Marinda

The first time I laid eyes on Marinda, it was an early afternoon in mid-September, sometime in the late 70s. My morning charter, a contingent from the local order of Keg Busters, had filled the fish box with blues and bass and themselves with at least 100 gallons of beer.

Their spokesman, Suds Saldowski, often said that they were charter members of the Pistol Club. In other words, they drink all day and piss till dawn.

My mate, Cleveland, as well as other mates, had returned to college. They could only work on weekends, which left everyone in our fleet somewhat short-handed from Monday to Friday till the end of the season in early October.

I was working in the stern of the Seawitch cleaning up a mess, when I look up to see a teenager looking down at my fish box.

"Sir," she said. "Do you have any fish for sale."

"I'm sure I do," I answered.

We almost always had fish left over and they, most of the time, went to Captain Lobster for bait. He in turn repaid us with the fruits of his labor. I looked in our bait tank to see 3 6-pound bluefish and a small bass.

"How much does one cost?" she asked peeking into the tank. "I got $2.20; is that enough to buy one?"

I took a long look at the kid. "No," I said. "But if you help me clean this boat, I will give you all these fish and show you how to clean them. How does that sound?"

At that instant it was like she was looking at all her presents under the Christmas tree. "Yes, sir," she said. "Can I help now?"

I nodded the affirmative and we made a deal as we worked: she would come down every day after high school to help me clean, and in exchange she could keep some of the leftover fish and get paid as well.

As the season was drawing to a close, I noticed that she had been given fish from several boats in our fleet. I wasn't paying too much attention to this, as I thought she was selling them.

However, Captain Lobster put me straight on that line of thought.

"She's not selling them. She cleans them, keeps the fillets, and I get the racks."

"Well, maybe she sells them to the restaurants and hotels?"

"No," said Captain Lobster. "She doesn't do that either."

"Well, what in the world does she do with them? Her and her family couldn't eat them all. I know that. She gets from 25 to 50 pounds a day from the fleet."

Captain Lobster looked at me with a grinning face. "She gives them away."

"What? That's right, Captain. She gives them away. She takes them to old people and folks that don't have a lot of money. She asks for nothing in return. My granddaughter told me that she belongs to a group of young people who go around to the farms, hotels, and restaurants and picks up what is ever leftover. They call themselves the Hunger Troopers."

I was surprised and delighted that her and her friends were making good use of a lot of leftover fish. I was even more pleased that she was doing a wonderful service to help people.

Marinda worked with us one more season. Late the following fall, shortly after we were in dry dock, I learned that she and her family moved off cape and settled someplace in the mid-west.

Time passed, and I had forgotten the pretty little girl until a decade and a half later, when on a bright May morning, I was told by one of the mates that some people wanted to see me.

"Well, tell them to come on down," I said.

She looked at me, "I don't think so, Captain. You best go up there."

I climbed the ramp and saw several nuns waiting at the top when a nun came to me with open arms and hugged me. I was astonished, surprised, and delighted at the same time. As I looked down at the smiling face of Sister Margaret Mary, my Marinda, of the Sisters of Charity.

Her life had changed for the better. She began helping a few individuals as a child and now she would help thousands.

"Do you remember the first time I came to your boat?"

I nodded in affirmation.

"You gave us a few fish to feed people. Now I keep thinking about the Bible story of the two loaves and five fish. The Lord multiplied and fed a lot of people."

"Well," I said. "Now through you he is doing it again, isn't he?"

Marinda smiled. "Yes, He certainly is."

Conclusion

~~~~~~~~~~

My home in Palmer, Massachusetts has a den with a rather unique book case. It contains 40 volumes of logbooks of the charter fishing vessel, Seawitch. Dated from 1967 to 2007, each volume represents one year of operation and each day of that year that we sailed. Each entry contains the pertinent information of that day, including weather, location, fish taken, time, tide, people who were aboard, and all of the events of that day. Though my memory sometimes fades, I don't worry about it, for all I have to do is open a log book and it will all be there for me again. I'll easily recall the people, the times, and the love we all shared for the sea.

I am proud of the fact that I was the first captain to hire young women to work on a professional charter boat on Cape Cod Bay. I hope you found the stories full of riveting revelations and unique adventures. Immerse yourself in another time and place with those who went to sea with the dolphins in the fire.

To paraphrase Emily Brontë, there is a place more restful than any sleep, it's a whisper in the wind and the rapture of the deep.

Author's Note

When I was still operating the charter boat Seawitch, people would ask me if I ever get tired and want to quit the business. They wondered why I didn't just fish for myself or give up the sea and do something different. I usually replied by reaching into my bag of stock answers with something like "my enlistment isn't up yet," or "you mean go to work for a living?" However, on rare occasions or in a moment of weakness, I told the truth, which was simply that I love the sea, fishing, and people. Being a charter boat captain allowed me to enjoy all three to the fullest.

Glossary

Barnstable Harbor: inlet 1/3 of the way down Cape Cod, Massachusetts

Billingsgate Shoal: popular location to troll for striped bass

Bow: front of the boat

Callahan Tunnel: old tunnel in Boston linking city to Logan Airport

Chain fall: a pulley with a chain, a lifting device

Cleat: metal tie-down device

Drag: device that administers tension to a reel

Eggheads: another word for someone who is nerdy, geeky, smart

Falstaff: a character from Shakespeare's books with very few morals

Filene's Basement: store with deep discounts arranged in an a slightly disorganized manner

Finest kind: the very best

Finger peers: docking facility that branches off from the main dock

Flying bridge: a cabin on some boats over the main helm for a second steering station

Gaff: long handle hook used to lift fish out of the water

Gunnels: sides of the boat

Helmsman seat: a seat located in the area in which a boat is steered

Henry Higgins: a character from the movie, *My Fair Lady*

Hull: the whole part of the boat in the water

Lures: artificial bait to attract fish

Mooring: stationary buoy anchored so a boat can be tied up to it

Mr. Wright: father of Orville and Wilbur Wright, inventors of the airplane

Panzer: German word meaning armor or tank

Phalanx: Greek term meaning unit position

Pile: large school of fish

Plugs: fishing lures

Plymouth: North of Cape Cod heading toward Boston, Massachusetts

Pots: lobster traps

Prop wash: turbulence from a ship's propeller

Pulpit: raised platform on the bow of a boat

Rigs: device for catching fish

Rip shit: another term for angry, pissed off

Saved: caught enough fish to get paid

Scuppers: holes on the back of the boat

Second string: 2nd position

Smote: hard strike

Starboard: right side of boat

Stern: back of the boat

Trolling: fishing with the boat in motion

Transom: another name for stern

Turn: type of bird

Wake: turbulence from a boat passing through the water

W. C. Fields: American comedian from early 1900s to 1940s

About the Author

~~~~~~~~~~~~~~~~

Captain Robert R. Singleton, PhD is a merchant marine captain and an-oceanographer who has spent well over 40 years at sea. He is also apri-vate pilot and an ex-paratrooper from the famed 101st AirborneDivision. Captain Singleton has authored several books and other articles,including "You'll Never Get Lost Again: Simple Navigation for Everyone,""The Standish Chronicles," and "Angels, Visions, and Gifts." He enjoyswriting, teaching, and many outdoor activities.